The Original Sin

THE
ORIGINAL
SIN

Incest and
Its Meaning

W. ARENS

New York   Oxford
OXFORD UNIVERSITY PRESS
1986

OXFORD UNIVERSITY PRESS

Oxford   New York   Toronto
Delhi   Bombay   Calcutta   Madras   Karachi
Petaling Jaya   Singapore   Hong Kong   Tokyo
Nairobi   Dar es Salaam   Cape Town
Melbourne   Auckland

and associated companies in
Beirut   Berlin   Ibadan   Nicosia

Published by Oxford University Press, Inc.,
200 Madison Avenue, New York, New York 10016

Oxford is a registered trademark of Oxford University Press

Library of Congress Cataloging-in-Publication Data
Arens, W., 1940–
The original sin.
Bibliography: p.   Includes index.
1. Incest—Cross-cultural studies.   I. Title.
HQ71.A73   1986   306.7'77   85-31080
ISBN 0-19-503754-5 (alk. paper)

2 4 6 8 10 9 7 5 3 1

Printed in the United States of America
on acid-free paper

For Diane

Preface

My curiosity with the subject of incest was piqued some time ago while doing the literary research for a book on the history and function of the idea of cannibalism. In the eventual publication (Arens 1979a) I concluded with fervor, but not without some trepidation, that there was little if any evidential reason to accept the prevailing folk and anthropological notion that man-eating was once a widespread human custom. As a result, when colleagues learned that I was interested in the present topic, they inquired if I were now going to deny the existence of incest in human affairs. In addition to misinterpreting the nature of my previous argument, this presumption reflects a gross misunderstanding of the nature of the present situation. The literature suggests quite clearly that as a rule intellectuals have either ignored or unintentionally denied the existence of incest in propounding their theories about the universality of the prohibition. The incest taboo, which has commanded most of the attention, and incest may be the opposite sides of the same coin. However, they are obviously not the same thing. This simple fact has been lost on many an erudite commentator. To be brief and explicit, this essay is concerned primarily with examining the practice, meaning, and significance of incest, rather than with its prohibition. The latter topic has been worried over by so many others and is considered here only with reference to the light it may shed on the deed itself.

The history of the incestuous image was linked with but then diverged from the cannibal notion. Formerly, the accusation that certain peoples in the past or distant present were engaged in both cannibalism and incest was quite common. These visions of the exotic other were popularly entertained in travellers' accounts for centuries. Thus Strabo wrote that the ancient Irish were inclined to eat their dead father and have sex with their living mother and sisters (1939:261). This sort of reporting about the sexual case of others remained in vogue for some centuries, until subsequently challenged by the armchair anthropology of the nineteenth century, which took issue with such an interpretation. The incestuous image was eventually done in by twentieth-century ethnographers, who encountered no societies characterized by indiscriminate sexual or marital behavior. Indeed, the often rather complex marriage systems reported on became a major focus of attention for those with a professional interest in other societies. In the process, incest slipped from view, remaining unattended to or at most only a nagging side issue. It was generally agreed in this century that all the world's peoples abided by some basic sexual restrictions. This veil of sexual modesty became the mark of humanity, in opposition to presumed animal behavior of a contrasting sort, while the sporadic appearance of cannibalism in other cultures continued to provide a dividing line between the savage and the civilized. Thus it was concluded that in all societies it was forbidden to have sex at the least with one's parent or child, but in some an individual was allowed to eat them after their demise. This is a rather odd and inexact view of human nature, but there it remains.

Our culture is not the only one to have linked up these notions of sexual and nutritional voraciousness in the same way. Travellers and, later, anthropologists would often note that a particular group of people held its neighbors in low regard because, it was avowed, they insisted on either marrying or eating their kin. The boundary between savage and civilized behavior within a particular culture can be represented in a similar fashion, as was demonstrated by the Kwakiutl of North America, with their former ritual of the "cannibal dance."

In a striking ceremony, a chosen individual appeared as the representation of a beast or an ogre lusting for human flesh, which leads him to bite those around him. He was joined in this stylized frenzy by his sexually taboo naked sister, carrying a corpse representing another basic taboo, that against eating human flesh. However, according to the description, even her lascivious dance could not distract him from this base desire. He eventually makes his choice between competing unnatural lusts by choosing the corpse for food, rather than his sister for sex. In a final dance sequence, others place a blood-soaked menstrual cloth over his face, which subdues him, since he has now apparently appeased all primal desires. After the ceremony, in which he has actually or symbolically confronted a variety of forbidden objects of desire, he is no longer considered human by others. He is then retaught all the basics of cultured life, as if he were a newborn child (Walens 1981:15–16).

Although not every society may join such representations in such an explicit and dramatic way as the Kwakiutl, this ceremony exemplifies some pervasive cultural images. When human beings in any place or form, which may include the printed word in our time, reflect upon the incest taboo, they are confronting a theme commonly believed to represent a baseline in the definition of human morality. The prohibition has such profound positive implications in its observation, and contrasting negative connotations in its violation, that neutrality is difficult to maintain when the topic is taken under advisement. This is likely the fate of any subject impinging on the definition of human nature. Thus, in reviewing the literature on the incest prohibition and allied subjects, the implicit a priori assumptions and subjective tone of many arguments are easily recognizable. This is not surprising for intellectual endeavors we would now characterize as moral philosophy, but the same quality is also often the case in contemporary social science, ideally characterized as a more neutral enterprise. Considering the history of an idea generally perceived as being intimately linked with the definition of human nature not surprisingly involves a confrontation with human nature in the form of academic treatises. As such, this is one of those problems which tests the intellectual mettle of each successive generation of social scientists and provides an encapsulated view of shifting visions of human nature. This would not be true if the matter had or could be resolved to everyone's satisfaction. Clearly this has not been the case. Consequently, following the train of thought on this worrisome subject also provides an insight into the culture of social science, which has been charged by our society with a formal interpretation of our nature.

On a more personal and lighter side, this exercise has provided the stimulating pleasure of mandating the time to read and consider the work of some illustrious predecessors in anthropology, who were recommended to me but surreptitiously avoided when I was a student. Delving into the past literature on this and related topics has its own fascination. The reader encounters as a typical example a three-volume study, running over a thousand pages, engaged in the running battle over whether "mother-right" preceded "father-right" in the dim past of humankind. This industriousness is startling enough in itself. Even more astounding is the fact that from today's perspective, less than a century later, it is deemed that there was nothing in the way of direct or reliable evidence from either history or primitive anthropology to support either contention. As a result, this admittedly fascinating problem has been dismissed as irrelevant rather than solved. Regrettably, it can only be assumed that a similar judgment awaits the objects of contemporary grand theory in the social sciences. However, it would be comforting to believe, since we now understand more of what is involved, that a future generation of scholars will conclude that we have learned something more than the art of brevity.

There have also been other rewards in the process of reading backwards, rather than only forwards. One could easily get the impression that a latent function of the incest taboo has been to test the limits of human intellectual ingenuity and imaginative fantasy. Every announced conqueror has voluntarily set out into the wasteland to confront this intellectual Gordian knot. Yet it seems reasonable to conclude today that none has made a clean cut, while others seem to have been intellectually impaired by the very experience of considering the topic. On the other hand, one also glumly learns that these individuals, sometimes glibly dismissed in textbooks for the error of their ways, were most often extremely learned, even though anthropology was usually their passionate avocation, rather than a profitable occupation. In their spare time earlier commentators mastered and reasonably discussed rather erudite matters, such as kinship and marriage systems, which today are considered to be very technical matters for specialists.

My intent is more modest than that of these predecessors, and even more limited in scope than contemporary intellectual fashion. As indicated, my principal concerns are with tracing the history of the thought on the prohibition, and then with commenting on incest itself. I do not offer a novel explanation for the taboo, even if that were still possible. Nonetheless, the engagement calls for a consideration of existing theories and approaches concerned with the prohibition, in order to make eventual sense of the deed. In thought and practice the restriction and deed are inextricably joined. My interest is not so much explanation as it is sorting out the variety of issues and rearranging them in order to gain an understanding of the problem. This procedure will entail trying to maintain, as far as possible, a neutral and nondeterminist position on some matters; but on others this will not always be the case. Therefore, rather than surreptitiously slipping into a position of advocacy, some suppositions should be stated at the outset.

First, the reasoning which follows gives initial credit to recent arguments and evidence from biology and ethology in the search for a comprehension of incest and its prohibition. This approach is not typical for contemporary social science. However, this is neither a unique procedure nor is it undertaken here without reservations. These qualms are at times concerned with objective matters, such as the reliability of the evidence and alternately with how this biological view of human nature impacts on more subjective conclusions having little regard for evidence. It is some consolation to me, though it may not have the same import for others, that I arrived at these positions in the course of considering the problem, rather than allowing them to preordain a conclusion. As with most social scientists, I am extremely wary of both the implications and errors of what has come to be known as sociobiology. I have noted these where warranted. Second, as a converse to the initial line of approach, I place greater emphasis than usual on the role of culture, in the form of human inventiveness, with regard to an understanding of incestuous behavior. In brief, it is suggested here that incest, rather than its avoidance, is a product of human culture. Finally, I have attempted to place these two often contentious views of human nature—the biological and cultural—together in a fashion which may offer some unique insights into the general problem.

The entire procedure means that I have on occasion gone out on a limb for the adventure of the exercise. As one colleague who has commented on this particular problem suggests, there is greater intellectual satisfaction in risking being wrong on an important subject than in being assured of being right on a trivial one (Chagnon 1981). Although no one could deny the exciting nature of such a challenge, it is still a dubious proposition. In point of fact, it is just as likely that, even on relatively minor matters, scholars are loath to offer their unqualified allegiance to each other. The pages of academic journals often give testimony to the fact that the two or three foremost scholars of the world rarely agree on even the insignificant. Therefore, it might be best to recast the theorem by suggesting that it may be more rewarding if others assume you are wrong on an important, rather than a minor, matter.

While on the subject of the peculiarities of academic culture, I should note some caveats. I have not recounted in the following pages all the recorded theories and their variations encountered in the course of reading. Lord Raglan's (1940) argument is a good, and often favorite, case in point. He was of the opinion that the emergence of the incest taboo might be laid in part to the "ancient superstition" that it is dangerous for a man to have sexual intercourse with a woman who lives on the same side of the stream as himself. Raglan must have been a self-assured and sensible gentleman-scholar, because as soon as he proposed the argument, he immediately doubted its own plausibility and seemed to wash his hands of the whole matter. As a result, I have felt no need to go into detail on this and similar propositions which have all the marks of intellectual despair.

Even one of the great masters of social science, Emile Durkheim, appears to have been uncharacteristically befuddled by this issue. In a relatively obscure publication (1963), he put forward the notion that the prohibition of incest came into effect because primitives believed that the spiritual essence of their totemic gods resided in the blood of their clan members. As a result, the males feared deflowering their female kin lest they come in contact with the divinity in the process. Thus they prohibited the deed we would call incest. Raglan's and Durkheim's arguments were much more erudite than I have rendered them here, even to the extent of posing some difficulties in following their complexities. Moreover, I believe that, although their lines of reasoning have little to offer in the way of explanation for the origin of the taboo as they propose, they do suggest some insights into the way in which cultures generate symbolic oppositions on the score of sexual behavior. However, since this conclusion was not their intention, it must be best for all concerned if their more detailed arguments on this topic remain obscure.

In the following pages I have also tried to set the record straight on the origin of certain theories on the origin of the incest taboo. Delving into a particular subject which has attracted so many commentators over the years inevitably leads to the discovery that an originally published idea often goes unnoticed, and then uncited in print by others. This suggests that, at this stage of the intellectual process on this subject, there may be no new ideas, only ignorance of what has already been written. This may be the case, particularly with a topic such as this one, which cuts across what are today a number of sub-specialized academic disciplines, ranging from genetics to ancient history. Omissions of some source material and errors of interpretation are inevitable, and the responsibility is mine, despite the expert assistance of many as I overstepped reasonable boundaries. Those who have offered their time, knowledge, and skills include Göram Aijmer, Diana Antos Arens, Paulette Chase, Ruth Cowan, John Fleagle, Norman Goodman, Michael Gramly, Gretchen Gwynne, David Hicks, Ivan Karp, Maria Messina, Graham Spanier, June Starr, Lawrence Taylor, Mari Walker, and Eviatar Zerubavel. Without them the task would have been more difficult and time-consuming, and my arguments substantially lacking in merit. My thanks are also due to the professional staff at the Stony Brook Libraries, particularly Nathan Baum, Leonore Brodie, Jacob Lipkind, Blossom Spitzer, Virginia Whitford and Jai Yun. Finally, William Curtis of Oxford University Press has been both helpful and encouraging in a most amiable way.

On the matter of style, my intent has been to write in a manner understandable to anyone interested in this fascinating subject. Those who may feel cheated by the experience of comprehension should refer to the notes, where I have appended most of my equivocations, qualifications, and obfuscations.

Stony Brook, N.Y.   W.A.
January 1986

Contents

The Original Sin

And the eyes of them both were opened,
and they knew that they were naked . . .

Genesis 3:7

CHAPTER 1

The Culture
of the Problem

Incest must indeed be reckoned as one of man's major
interests in life.   LESLIE WHITE, 1948

IF THE ABOVE is correct, then I am about to consider a stale topic.
Every library seems to contain shelves of books, articles, chapters,
pamphlets, and encyclopedia entries on incest. Moreover, the subject has attracted the recognized masters of the natural and social
sciences, including Darwin, Freud, Frazer, Durkheim, and even the
deceased Marx, via his notebooks and the living Engels.[1] There
have been others from the past, such as Maine, Morgan, and Tylor,
and in our time most notably Lévi-Strauss, and even these do not
do justice to the list. Raising this topic yet again might therefore be
considered both futile and presumptuous. What more could be
said that is worth listening to, and what kind of apology should
be offered for the exercise?

But the image of accumulated wisdom is an illusion and, as such,
poses an intriguing problem in itself. For Freud, incest was a historical or contemporary fantasy rather than reality; for the others,
the origin of the incest *taboo*, rather than incest itself, was the
focus of their considerable attention. Not a one considered incest
itself except as an aside. Nor has this situation changed today: one
need only turn to an encyclopedia entry on "Incest," or the pages
listed under the same rubric in the index of a textbook, for a syn-
opsis of the existing theories on the very opposite: the prohibition
of incest. Compounding this situation are the numerous books and
articles with the word "incest" in their titles, which again turn out

to be considerations of the prohibition in old and new light.[2] We seem to be drawn repeatedly to the topic of incest, but unconsciously discuss its antithesis, assuming each time that we have satisfied our original curiosity and intent. The belief that incest has already been systematically confronted, explored, and understood could not be further from reality.

This characterization of the intellectual atmosphere surrounding the subject of incest is not meant to disparage those cited, for the prohibition is as important to consider as the practice. This interpretation is offered merely to draw attention to the cloudy nature of the subject. Both theoretically and ethically, incest has eluded our grasp, and the intellectual twist this demanded has gone unrecognized. Surely it is just as reasonable to ask why incest exists and then, having provided some rationale, to explore its meaning in human affairs. The obscurity that prevails belies Foucault's dictum that during the Victorian era sex was forced out into the open to lead what he calls "a discursive existence." At the same time, the present situation supports his contention that despite "long-winded" discourse, sex was still "the secret" (1978:33–35). In effect, the massive amount of attention paid to the subject of the incest taboo has meant a denial of incest. Thought has been controlled by discourse.

I have used the word "theoretical" in these lines so as not to deny the availability of a related literature on incest of a quite different nature. Today the outpourings of incest victims, their therapists, social workers, and journalists, all of whom are confronting the actual behavior, are now unavoidable.[3] However, their intent is often cathartic and explicitly subjective, as they seek to find some meaning and responsibility for the failure of the prohibition in our own society.

There are also the occasional pieces by historians, prehistorians, and anthropologists, commenting on perceived violations of the taboo in other times and cultures. Again, these instances are considered primarily in light of the question of why an assumed universal has failed to hold in a particular instance. The prohibition, the positive aspect of this behavioral complex, again takes precedence, as these discussions typically deflate into critiques of existing explanations for the origin or function of the taboo. Rather than these oblique confrontations with incest as psychological abnormality or historical oddity, what is required is the same sort of perspective to incest itself as has been applied so readily to its opposite. This means agreeing to the fact that incest exists as both a theoretical and practical problem, deserving of explanation. Such a confession will demand the recognition of anomaly, disorder, and the negative in human affairs, rather than uniformity, order, and the positive, which is implied by the prohibition. In addition, this admission will require the sorting out and evaluation of some crucial concepts and facts that bear on both the deed and its prohibition. Many of these are assumed to be well understood, but this is not the case.

First, what is implied by the word "incest"? According to the standard reference, *Notes and Queries in Anthropology*, incest ". . . is sexual intercourse between individual's related in certain prohibited degrees of kinship" (113). This seems simple enough, but most will recognize that this definition intimates that some societies allow sexual relations between certain individuals that others will not abide. Thus there is an immediate complexity built into the definition, to be considered in due course. However, there is an even more basic problem involved, for Needham (1974) instructs us that the very term "incest" as an English linguistic concept is culture bound. In typically provocative fashion, he points out that the word derives from the Latin *castum*, meaning "chaste." Thus the English rendering connotes impurity, but this is not directly comparable to the meaning of the term for the same act even in other Germanic languages, where it involves the idea of "blood shame." Going still further afield for examples, Needham remarks on the notions of disorder in Chinese and repugnant in Indonesian, conveyed in these languages by the concept we translate simply and uniformly as incest.

Clearly, the same meaning is not implied in these contexts, so there is no singularity of thought on this matter. There may be an element of negativism conveyed by the notions of impurity, shame, disorder, and repugnance, but these are not comparable in other regards. In light of these distinctions, Needham concludes that incest prohibitions do not compose a homogenous social class.[4] In other words, the *incest* prohibition is not universal, since the very concept is culture-bound. To dismiss this as formalistic quibbling would be to overlook a major point: significant cultural variability characterizes a concept that is normally expressed in English as if there were uniformity of thought.

Finally, in this context it should be noted that the ethnographic record suggests there are some societies that lack explicit concepts of incest (Needham 1974:65–66). This means that certain people have no specific word for sexual relations between prohibited relatives. Such societies do have behavioral rules that exclude such activity, and if the deed were to occur it would no doubt be deemed illicit. On the other hand, they have no apparent past nor present experience with such behavior. Thus it is not possible to conclude that there is anything resembling a uniform response to violations of what we call incest taboo. Some societies are very tolerant of or oblivious to such behavior, express no collective horror, while others take drastic action in cases of sexual relations between individuals to which we would have no objection. The Mossi of Upper Volta, for example, admit to no cases of what to them would be absurd behavior. They can conceive of neither natural nor supernatural consquences, except for possible embarrassment to those involved, if such behavior became known to others. In contrast are the Jalé of New Guinea, whose broad view of prohibited sexual partners includes any member of one's moiety (a series of linked clans forming one-half of the population). Sexual activity between members of the same social division is punishable by death for both parties. However, on occasion, the male can be reprieved by undergoing a ritual involving eating a coprophagous sausage, that is, a pig's bladder stuffed with human and animal excrement (Fiske 1982). Obviously, the recognition and definition of, and response to, prohibited partners and sexual behavior are variable matters. If incest per se is not universal in any sense, what can be said about the meaning and, more important, the assumed ubiquity of the taboo? Here again, the issue is not simple.

The second word in the familiar phrase "incest taboo" suffers from even greater misunderstanding. In its original sense, as well as in terms of existing secondary meanings, the word *tabu*, borrowed from the Polynesian language of Tonga, does not mean "prohibited in an absolute sense." According to *The Oxford English Dictionary*, *tabu* originally meant "set apart for or consecrated to a special purpose; restricted to the use of a god, king or chiefs, while forbidden to general use. . . ." This definition accorded with the situation in those highly stratified societies where certain activities were prohibited to one class or group while allowed for another. Thus *tabu* implies that the behavior in question is expected to be engaged in by some. And, in point of fact, some of these island societies, as well as others in different parts of the world, did enjoin their political rulers to enter into prohibited marriages forbidden to all others.[5] Whether or not sex and reproduction were involved are altogether different matters and must be considered apart. Suffice it to say for now that, from a linguistic perspective, the incest taboo is not a universal, for no other reason than the fact that there are some societies, such as our own, that prohibit the deed entirely. Putting it the other way around, technically an incest taboo may be said to prevail only in a society where some individuals are either allowed to or actually enjoined to marry, and in which, simultaneously, others may not do the same without running the risk of sanctions.

All of this may produce a mild figurative, if not literal, headache. I am also aware that anyone who insists upon literality for its own sake is looking for trouble in the form of having one's argument dismissed out of hand for petty contentiousness. Thus, for the sake of literary convention, I will continue to use the phrase "incest taboo" with the understanding that it conveys more complexity than is usually assumed. This semantic concern is not meant to replace common linguistic currency, where the word "taboo" has come to mean prohibition. The intent is to make a simpler and more reasonable point about cultural systems: if some societies exhibit an explicit rule in the form of a prohibition against certain sexual behavior for all, while others have the same injunction for most but expect others to contravene it, and still others have no such verbal precept, then we are clearly dealing with cultural variation rather than uniformity. The crucial failure to recognize cultural differences implied by the statement that "the incest taboo" is universal with some exceptions will simply not do. Such a proposition fails to do justice to the problem by sweeping away crucial complexities at the first step of consideration. Any argument derived from such a restricted view of what is at issue must eventually come to naught. This is immediately obvious in the instance of past theories based on the assumption that sexual relations between members of the nuclear family are "instinctually" avoided. A similar problem exists for arguments that equally mysteriously and obliviously suggest that "genetic programming" is at issue in considering the origin and function of the incest prohibition.

In sum, despite the opinion to the contrary contained in myriad textbooks, it is essential to recognize that the incest taboo is not universal and to proceed from there. This is a more complex proposition to entertain than we are accustomed to, but then so is the problem. This recognition of cultural complexity may not result in a better explanation, but it will allow for a better appreciation of what has to be accounted for in the course of the investigation of both the prohibition and the deed. Incest and its prohibition or avoidance are not the same, but it would do well to consider the one in light of the other. The opposite approach, which avoids a confrontation with the deed, is typical, but it has produced only lingering confusion and dispute.

Dismissing the varied linguistic connotations and considering the behavior only, it is safe to postulate that incest—as sexual relations between prohibited kin—takes place regularly. Outside the nuclear family, permissible sexual behavior is a matter of cultural preference, since, as noted, there is no universal agreement on this score. However, there is far greater conformity when it comes to considering sexual relations between primary relatives, such as parents and offspring or brother and sister. These "core prohibitions" or avoidance patterns (Cohen 1964) have far greater cross-cultural applicability. At the same time, such rules or standards are not always heeded in practice, since incest in the nuclear-family context also takes place.

Thus it is best for the moment to ignore the welter of theories attempting to account for its opposite, and to consider incest alone to determine what is entailed. Without necessarily being explicit, commentators have typically recognized two different types of incest: unsanctioned violations of some standard which are not condoned by society, and sanctioned violations of the same standard which are enjoined for a political elite. The illicit instances are widespread and would include those in our own and related socities; the other form, though rarer, is not uncommon in the historical and anthropological record. Well-known cases of condoned incest include the royalty of ancient Egypt, Thailand, Hawaii, and the Incan state of Peru. Examples from sub-Saharan Africa have also been haphazardly included in this category (see van den Berghe and Mesher 1980). In addition, there was the peculiar but well-documented occurrence of incestuous marriages among a significant portion of the Egyptian middle class during the Roman era, which extended from the first to the fourth centuries A.D. (Middleton 1962; Hopkins 1980). This is a particularly bedeviling instance, for—lacking other examples—it comprises a unique class and thus must be considered a legitimate ethnographic and historical oddity.

Nor can this prevalence of incestuous marriages be dismissed as either antisocial or as a peculiar prerogative of royalty. Instead it presents incest-prohibition theorists of all persuasions with a nagging problem. Sometimes this is resolved by consigning the information to an exasperated aside or, more cleverly, to a footnote, but this is unsatisfactory, since it highlights the rich diversity of human custom, obscured by purveying the notion of the universality of the incest taboo.

The preceding paragraphs have quietly introduced a major distinction that now must be explicitly addressed. I refer to the fact often noted by Fox (e.g., 1983:54–55) that, despite their association, there is an enormous difference between sex and marriage.[6] He remarks with insight and humor that, although this difference may be obvious to the typical teen-ager, it has been lost on some great academic theorists, who conflate the two when considering the incest prohibition. Fox draws attention to those societies, usually characterized by premarital sexual freedom, that allow individuals related through a common ancestor, such as cousins, to engage in sexual relations, but simultaneously prohibit them from marrying. This may seem an odd arrangement, since our ideals equate sex and marriage, but such a union is by no means universal.

This issue is raised in order to clarify the distinction between rules of exogamy, which govern the suitability of a marriage partner, and incestuous regulations, which govern permissible sexual behavior.[7] Fox's principal concern is to indicate that any theory attempting to explain incest prohibitions by erroneously considering mar-

riage rules unknowingly circumvents the problem by considering a
different issue, rather than accounting for the one initially raised.
This has not been uncommon. Upon reflection, however, it is clear
that sex does not always imply marriage. Less obvious and more
difficult to entertain is the possibility that marriage may not involve
sex. Again, as Fox notes: "No society (I believe) is bloody-minded
enough to ban sex from marriage . . ." (1983:54). There is no good
reason to debate this point for human populations in general (indeed, it would be difficult to imagine the continued existence of a
society if this were the case). However, in the examples of condoned, presumably incestuous marriages cited above there is the
possibility that sex need not be involved. To conclude invariably
that it is would be to fall into the opposite trap of assuming that
marriage and sex always go together. When dealing with cultural
anomalies, such as the expected behavior of royalty, it might be wise
to consider the possibility that their behavior may vary from the
norm in other ways. In point of fact, sex, and its equally important
but distinct correlate of reproduction, may not have been a feature
of these royal unions. This possibility has been cogently considered
(Bixler 1982a), and must be entertained in assessing any explanation for the incest prohibition. But this is not to overlook the possibility that such an arrangement symbolized the violation of sexual
norms.

There would seem to be little reason to assume a similar context
for the Egyptian middle-class marriages previously mentioned, but
here it must be remembered that this is a unique case, as opposed
to the marriage patterns of royalty from so many different eras and
parts of the world. Royal unions are concerned with formulating
and transmitting an everlasting cultural message about the nature
of the right to rule, while the Egyptian middle-class instance appears to have been a transitory response to foreign domination.

Despite these potential disclaimers, it remains that, at one extreme, incest in the form of both actual sexual intercourse and reproduction does take place in some societies in which it is explicitly
prohibited. In addition, symbolic and/or actual incestuous marriages have also been reliably recorded in human history. A fruitful
consideration of existing theories directed at making sense of incest
avoidance or prohibition would be impossible if these facts were

not kept in the forefront.[8] Bearing in mind that all sorts of behaviors that we and others interpret as irregular or prohibited nevertheless take place regularly and frequently permits a different appreciation of existing theories. More important, acknowledging this fact permits insight into certain common but unstated assumptions on which popular explanations for the prohibition of incest are based.

In addition to the social varieties of what we deem incestuous behavior, which include institutionalized and noninstitutionalized exceptions, there is also the need to consider a range of interpersonal possibilities. In the case of royalty, all possible heterosexual variations of incest have been recorded, although there is good reason to suspect that mother son incest has always been purely sym bolic in those African states in which there has been a special relationship between the two.[9] In societies such as our own, with a stated prohibition against sexual contact between members of the nuclear family (except for the spouses), the record includes all possible homosexual and heterosexual instances.

Homosexuality in the family is much the rarer and involves other sexual prohibitions unrelated to the problem at hand, so it is best left to one side. However, it should be noted that some societies in New Guinea have institutionalized homosexuality for young males. Interestingly, the participants are expected to abide by the same prohibtions on partnerships governing heterosexual relationships, which they enter into via marriage at a later age (see Herdt 1981). In effect, this means they must avoid sexual liaisons with their brothers as well as all other male members of their descent group. This implies, in passing, that a society may take into consideration matters other than reproduction in deciding on proper sexual partners. This observation provides some support for the common assumption that physical or biological factors are irrelevant in prompting the emergence of the incest prohibition. Obviously in these New Guinea societies the sexual relationships in question are not expected to produce offspring, yet the participants still abide by certain restrictions.

Heterosexual possibilities, which are the main concern, include overt sexual activity between sister and brother, father and daughter, and mother and son. Although all three instances have been documented for our society, there is some disagreement about their frequency. Incest was downgraded by Kinsey as a relatively rare experience, one that "occurs more frequently in the thinking of clinicians and social workers than it does in actual performance" (1948: 558), but lately others have not been so sanguine. In a more recent publication, for example, Herman (1981:12) suggests that one out of every hundred females has had a "sexual experience" with either her father or stepfather. Commentators often fail to agree on the incidence of incest or even on terms, because the "experience" is often not consistently spelled out in detail, prohibiting comparison. But some reports (e.g., Morton 1961) indicate incontrovertibly that actual sexual intercourse sometimes does take place, with resulting pregnancy, so there is no possibility of denying the existence of such behavior in all of its variations. The consensus of opinion seems to be that father-daughter incest is the most common violation of the taboo in our society (Herman 1981).

There is a problem with rushing to conclusions on this score, for despite the fact that it may often go unreported, father-daughter incest is more than likely to be the variety most often entered in the public record. The father is still considered the authority figure in the Western household, so that if he fails in his responsibilities, recourse is usually achieved by seeking the assistance of public agencies. In addition, society also judges the adult male to be the offender, since this accords with our notions regarding the instigation of and responsibility for sexual behavior. The opposite instance, involving the mother-son dyad, presents greater difficulties, since deciding on the perpetrator and the victim is a more confusing matter. In any event, this kind of incest is likely to be resolved, however arduously, within the family, and more often finds its way into the psychological literature, rather than the public record.

Brother-sister sexual conduct of any sort, which some consider the most prevalent form of incest (Gephard 1965), has a similar outcome. Since both authority figures are uninvolved, they are presumably prone to take immediate remedial action, rather than to seek aid from agencies that might hold them to be at fault for failing to meet their domestic responsibilities.

This inventory of possibilities was not undertaken to determine statistical validity, but rather to suggest that society recognizes difterences in the matter of sexuality between primary kin. The varying responses in our society accord well with what is generally apparent in other cultures, where there are differential evaluations of real or hypothetical incestuous possibilities. Although there is no way of enumerating or assessing actual incidence, most cultures would probably consider father-daughter and brother-sister sexuality as the more feasible, responding with greater incredulity when it comes to mother-son sexual activity. This situation is so unsettling as to confound many other categories of experience concerned with the style of proper relationships between the generations and genders.

Finally, the various potential constellations and their incidence suggest we entertain the possibility of different origins and functions for the prohibition or avoidance of sexual relations between members of the same nuclear family. It may be that no existing explanation can be shown to hold equally well for all the different possibilities. Incest avoidance or prohibitions may not admit to a single unified understanding. Therefore it might be more reasonable to consider the arguments in terms of these long-ignored variables. More important, it would be rash to dismiss any one argument for failing to hold for all incestuous relationships. And just as one pronouncement on this score may not legitimately be dismissed for failing to explain extensions of prohibitions, the same may well hold for a focus on the nuclear family. The relationships and experiences encompassed within this group are radically varied, rather than homogenous.

A matter of less subtlety is the now increasingly obvious fact that incest not only exists but does so in a variety of forms. This statement may seem all too obvious to bear repetition, but its verity and significance has consistently failed to make an impression on those concerned with explanations for incest prohibition. If incest had more often been recognized as a prominent feature of humantiy, we might have been spared some misdirected and tortuous arguments from those who have chosen to ignore this uncomfortable reality. Instead of having the solution to the problem avoid them, many previous commentators have managed more often than not to avoid a confrontation with the problem. Yet this seemingly inexplicable blind spot is a key element in uncovering any number of hidden ideas in existing commentaries on the subject of human nature which inform their interpretation of the incest prohibition. Before moving on to an estimation of such ephemeral topics as the epistemology and social theory of others, it makes good sense to be as explicit as possible in setting out the procedures and propositions that will guide this study.

In essence, what follows is an essay in the sense of a test and evaluation of existing material to determine the value of its intellectual content. The process involves the sometimes detailed consideration of the findings of different academic disciplines ranging from human genetics to the mating patterns of nonhuman primates. No apology can be offered for the welter of sometimes disparate facts that emerge. These are part of the terrain, and there is no safe way to avoid the difficulties. However, it is possible to provide a clearer vision of the final destination.

The conclusions arrived at here intially propose the adoption of some recently reinvigorated ideas concerned with the origin of the incest prohibition. Specifically this involves accepting the veracity of the long-standing hypothesis that the rule against incest is best understood as the eventual outcome of an innate human avoidance. This conclusion is offered in conjunction with a more novel view of the origin of incest which has lacked for an explanation. Putting the two parts of the problem in order, it is suggested that the relatively low incidence of incest among humans is ultimately derived from and conforms with our animal nature. Simply put, incest is avoided among humans. Alternatively it is proposed that the occurrence of the deed in whatever form it takes is ultimately derived from the cultural ingenuity of our species. Such conclusions imply that what we deem moral on this issue is the consequence of an inherent trait also found among other species. Thus the regular absence of incest in human affairs has nothing to do with basic ethical considerations or the cultural advance of our species over others. In contrast, the incestuous deed, universally judged to be immoral, is defined here as a product of our unique capacity to supersede natural inclinations. According to this interpretation incest, rather than its absence, is the unsightly but nonetheless true mark of humanity, culture, and civilization.

The avoidance-of-incest argument is a contentious but current one which has been seriously entertained for almost a century. This line of reasoning, however, contradicts the basic assumption that we are directly responsible for the propagation and continued maintenance of a basic moral standard. This element of the argument is unappealing, and as such often evokes a strong negative response. The second proposition on the origin of incest, which intimates that we must seek in our unique human nature the explanation for the violation of this standard, is even more contentious, but has never been seriously entertained. The opposing (and admittedly more popular) views on both matters conjure up a more satisfying vision of human nature. In Needham's (1983) terms it conveys all the tranquility of an axiom, and as such deserves considerable attention to the quality of the supporting evidence. Prevailing wisdom is not always a paradigm of rationality and veracity.

What is offered in part, then, is a revisionary view of human nature, based upon the consideration of incest and the existing evaluations of its prohibition. The unfamiliar vision of ourselves which emerges is achieved by drawing out that which has long lain hidden in the human consciousness. As such, the results could also be deemed an essay in the anthropology of evil. However, the unseemly behavior at issue is characteristic not of others nor of the supernatural, but of our own kind. Incest is a failing we have been loath to recognize in ourselves, let alone confess to others. Entertaining such a notion about the source of the deed requires the acceptance of what has been carefully denied. This resolution is achieved only through a careful consideration of implicit assumptions and a sorting out of all the attending issues on this subject. Paradoxically some of the (presumably) most basic questions seem to be open to a variety of conflicting explanations, while more complicated issues seem to be agreeably amenable to a single unstated strand of thought. Thus, for example, one would reasonably expect that whether or not incest has negative effects on reproduction would be a matter of consensus, while more basic assumptions about the existence of the prohibition would be a matter of serious dispute. But this is not the case, and hence it would be best to let few issues go unconsidered. It will not be necessary to undertake new research on either incest or its prohibition, but rather to consider carefully what is already conceded and then draw an unavoidable conclusion about the human capacity to define and engage in evil.

CHAPTER 2

The Nature
of the Problem

. . . Scientists are destroyers of myths.

ELIAS, 1978

THE CRUCIAL QUESTION at hand is ostensibly more neutral than most others which impinge upon this subject. What exactly are the physical consequences of reproduction by primary kin? The concern then is with inbreeding, rather than the value-laden notion of incest. This is an objective matter, for in and of themselves physiological processes pay no heed to subjective considerations. The human intellect may ponder them from a moral perspective, but this is a distinct concern. The existing conclusions on inbreeding may also be used in preparing an explanation for the prohibition or avoidance of sex among family members, but this is also only a related matter. Moreover, the same data have been relied upon both to support and deny a single explanation on the biological contribution to the general absence of inbreeding among humans. The moral, ethical, and theoretical implications of this subject are complex. The initial concern is only slightly less so, due to the human ingenuity to pose and repose the same question and answer it from different perspectives. The human body and mind themselves make for an intriguing marriage and consequence.

One would assume, and even hope, that this was a straightforward issue, easily resolved by either a simple positive or negative statement. As intimated, this is not the case, for there are indeed answers, rather than an answer, to the question of the effects of inbreeding and outbreeding. Part of the problem stems from the fact that, as a rule, humans, especially primary kin, do not inbreed. Con-

16

sequently, there are only limited data on consanguineous mating
that might be of assistance to social theorists as they reflect on the
absence of incest. Furthermore, biologists and geneticists are not as
concerned with this issue, which has compelled the attention of
anthropologists and sociologists. There is also the likelihood that
the experts are aware enough of the complexities to exercise reticence, where others more removed from the discipline might demonstrate less caution. Whatever the reason, these scientists often do
not say one way or the other what social scientists want to hear on
the matter of the biological effects of incest. To suggest as a result
that science is divided on this issue would be an oversimplification.
There is a great degree of uniformity of thought on the respective
implications of inbreeding and outbreeding. The best procedure involves an attempt to understand these prevailing ideas, rather than
adopting a position of misrepresentation or intellectual naivete, with
the suggestion that the matter is unsettled.

The simplest strategy is to consider those few studies which provide some data on the immediate biological implications of close
inbreeding, and subsequently to move outward to other literature
which considers the same results for inbreeding among more distantly related individuals, such as cousins. The former instances involve sexual intercourse and eventual reproduction as the consequence of violations of a prohibition, so that the data are severely
limited. The latter studies do not necessarily implicate a contradiction of rules, since cousin marriage of various degrees is often an
acceptable practice in our society and others. As a consequence, the
relevant information is much more extensive. Taken together, the
studies manifest a statistical trend for inbreeding and allow for com-
parisons with evidence on outbreeding.

On the score of reproduction among members of the same nuclear family, there are two principal studies. The first (Adams and
Neel 1967 and Adams et al. 1967) carefully considered eighteen
confirmed cases of offspring of incestuous unions[1] put up for adoption. Twelve children were the consequence of brother-sister com-
binations, and the remaining six the issue of father-daughter sexual
relations. The condition of these offspring was then compared to a
control group composed of a similar number of children born outside of marriage by eighteen other females closely matched in terms

of age, race, stature, weight, intelligence, and socioeconomic status.[2] The research team determined that only seven of the eighteen incestuous children could be considered physically or intellectually normal at the age of six months, and thus recommended for adoption. Of the remaining eleven, three had died, while the other eight suffered from some degree of morbidity or mental incapacity, such as severe retardation and/or cleft lip, seizures, and bone deformity. None of the comparison children had died or suffered from physical or mental incapacity, except for one with a congenital deformity. These factors led to the conclusion that the higher proportion of defective children was due to the negative genetic effects of inbreeding (Adams et al. 1967:142). It bears repeating that those involved in the study were also confronting the practical matter of adoption, as opposed to academic considerations alone.

A second study, by Seemanová (1971), confirmed these results in an interesting research fashion, since she was able to compare a group of incestuous children ($n = 161$) to their half siblings ($n = 95$) by the same mothers. In this case, there were eighty-eight offspring from father-daughter incest, seventy-two born of brothers and sisters, and one as the result of rare mother-son incest. The rates of prenatal, neonatal, and infant mortality were all higher among the inbred offspring, in comparison to their half siblings, who were the consequence of outbreeding. In addition, the inbreed study group had higher rates of congenital malformation and mental retardation than the control group of children. Seemanová points out that as congenital defects these consequences could not be attributed to poor health care at the prenatal or postnatal stages. Thus she concludes that ". . . the data presented here show an unmistakable effect of inbreeding on infant mortality, congenital malformations and intelligence level" (1971:118). Finally, a third, less elaborate, study of seven children of brothers and sisters and six of fathers and daughters produced findings consistent with the above conclusions. By the age of four to six years, three children had died of congenital defects, one was severely retarded, and four had measurably subnormal intelligence. Thus of the thirteen children, only five were deemed "normal" by the investigator (Carter 1967:436).

The results of this research on the immediate effects of consanguinity are quite clear. In all three instances more than half of the closely inbred offspring were considered to be physically or mentally subnormal. A smaller proportion of the children were not defective, indicating that inbreeding in and of itself does not necessarily produce an inferior product. What becomes apparent, though, is an aspect of what geneticists refer to as "inbreeding depression"— a reduction in the viability and thus potential fertility of offspring as the result of reproduction among close consanguines.

The consequences for the next generation of more distant inbreeding patterns, as with cousins of some degree, which is more widespread even among large populations, indicates a similar result.[3] In an overview of this research, Morton (1961) notes that early geneticists recognized that some rare human diseases increased among the progeny of such consanguineous marriages, even though the parents were not similarly affected. This trend was also a consistent, though less evident, research finding of subsequent investigations into consanguineous marriages.[4] Therefore, Morton concludes that morbidity, that is, illness among offspring, increases with inbreeding, even among more distantly related consanguines such as cousins (1961:274).

The issue of decreased fertility rates as the result of mortality among the offspring is not as apparent or as clear-cut when compared to the resulting data on reproduction among primary kin. Although the death rate for the children of cousin marriage is slightly higher (four percent in one study), there is also a corresponding net increase in the number of live births for this group, when compared to the general population (Schull and Neel 1965 and 1972). The authors suggest that this increased fertility may well be the result of "reproductive compensation" as married couples in this group attempted to make up for the increased infant mortality rates.[5]

In general, on the issue of the reproductive effects of cousin marriage, it is possible to conclude that the immediate risks to progeny are measurable, but statistically small when compared to the figures on outbreeding. (Cavalli-Sforza and Bodmer 1971:765). In addition, this sort of consanguineous mating pattern has no apparent negative effect on the distinct but related matter of population growth. However, the same conclusion cannot be maintained when the effects of closer inbreeding are scrutinized. In these instances of reproduction among family members, the negative effects for the offspring are all too apparent and severe. In light of the extremely high mortality and morbidity rates, it may be assumed that there would be similar dsyfunctional consequences for population growth.

There is some additional relevant evidence to consider on the potential effects of some degree of consanguinity on the offspring among highly inbred populations. Many of these studies are unsystematic and highly impressionistic, especially on the subjective issue of the intellectual ability of an inbred population (see Roberts 1967). The interdisciplinary research effort of McKusick and his associates on the Amish of Pennsylvania stands out in strong contrast to much of the other literature, and deserves careful consideration. The original Amish sect originated in Berne, Switzerland, in 1693. In 1723, a number of members emigrated to what is now eastern Pennsylvania and established a new community. The members do not marry outside of sectarian boundaries and rarely accept new members, which has led to the formation of "genetic isolates" traceable to founding married couples in Europe (Cross and Mc-Kusick 1978:29).

At the time of the research in 1973, all but three of the 1850 extant married couples in Lancaster were referred to as "demonstrably consanguineous" to the extent that each couple had a genetic relationship which was closer than that of second cousins (Mc-Kusick et al. 1978a:66). This intense degree of consanguinity was maintained, despite obvious efforts on the part of the population to mitigate its effects, as evidenced by the total absence of first-cousin and uncle-niece unions. However, there were 250 married couples who were second cousins several times over, so that the genetic relationship was actually equal to that of first cousins (McKusick et al. 1978b). In this genetic setting, five congenital disorders were isolated, including some previously undetected ones. This condition was deduced to be a consequence of an inbreeding pattern which allows for the recognizable appearance of abnormal physical features. This included Ellis-van Creveld Syndrome, manifested by dwarfism, polydactyly (extra digits), dystrophy of the fingernails, and partial hairlip (McKusick et al. 1978b:125). Although some of the other effects of inbreeding may be internal, and thus discernible only by sophisticated medical technology, it is clear that inbreeding will generate some obviously undesirable physical types.

In any event, among this sort of highly interbred population, a portion of the offspring will suffer from a variety of negative defects. This situation conforms to what had already been demonstrated for other types of inbreeding.

All the above suggests quite clearly that consanguineous reproduction may have some extremely deleterious consequences for a segment of the progeny, but the same will not be the case for all. An explanation for this differential response to the same process requires a more technical consideration of the problem, since, as noted, inbreeding by itself has no single effect. However, consanguineous reproduction does increase the chances of the transmission of recessive genes, which appear in the offspring when both parents are carriers of this trait. Again this will have no uniform consequence, since recessive genes may control the appearance of either negative or positive physical features. The viability problem of the offspring is the result of the fact that the existence of more recessive than dominant genes has negative implications (McKusick 1964:36). Therefore, an inbreeding population allows for the transmission of recessive genes to a greater extent than an outbreeding one. The consequence is an overall increase in morbidity and mortality to the offspring. In short, through a complicated process of genetic transmission, inbreeding will necessarily be harmful to a proportion of the physical products. Therefore, incest, if it were to result in reproduction, would also be more likely than not to have negative consequences for a particular child.

This reliable information is not meant to imply in more dubious fashion that at some time in the dim past of human history the recognition of these concrete physical manifestations among the offspring led to the avoidance or prohibition of incest. This is a familiar and hallowed argument in social science. As usually advanced it has serious defects, including some unrelated to the specific issue just considered. This review of the evidence on the effects of what may and is likely to occur with inbreeding of any sort was undertaken to indicate that the results are not controversial or debatable. These are the established facts of modern genetics. If this is the case, how then is it possible to interpret a statement such as that encountered in an anthropology textbook, when the origin of the presumed universal taboo is being considered: "The argu-

ment that inbreeding is biologically deleterious has been put to
rest . . ." (Vivelo 1978:215). Marvin Harris, the author of another
popular introduction to the subject, writes: "Contrary to popular
opinion, close inbreeding in small populations is not necessarily
deleterious for the population" (1975:327).

The response to the latter statement is simple. Popular opinion
is not concerned with what happens with inbreeding in "small populations," nor, I suspect, overly anxious about the effects on large
populations either. If popular opinion is concerned with anything,
it is with what happens when two closely related people get married
and have babies. Collective thinking on this matter, in terms of
genetic processes and statistical evidence, may be a bit fuzzy, but it
is essentially correct: it is probably not advisable for the sake of
their offspring. However, whether or not it is functional or dysfunctional for a "population" to inbreed is another matter entirely.
Therefore, the authors cited above are not incorrect in their conclusions. However, they are posing and responding to a different
question than the one previously considered here. In point of fact,
when a population is at issue, the matter is a different one entirely,
and the question of inbreeding has to be treated as such, rather than
confused with other issues.

Inbreeding for the offspring is clearly disadvantageous. They experience significantly higher degrees of mortality and morbidity in
the form of congenital defects. Whether or not inbreeding is also
disadvantageous for a population in the sense of exercising a negative check on its growth rate over an extended period is a different
and more complex issue. The statistics to support either contention
are unavailable, so there is some disagreement on this issue. However, the theoretical argument on how inbreeding may not have an
adverse long-term effect on a population is relatively simple.

A hypothetical inbreeding population promotes homozygosity,
which allows for the appearance of recessive genes. As noted, these
are most often disadvantageous for an individual. As a consequence
of the serious negative effects on the offspring, they are less likely to
reach maturity and, if so, to reproduce. These consequences eliminate the maladaptive characteristics from the population's gene
pool in relatively short order. This may or may not result in an immediate effect on the population as a whole, since, as indicated,

there is the possibility of compensation by the parents, with increased fertility as a response to infant mortality. However, the elimination of the recessive genes entailed by such inbreeding will enhance the chances of population growth in subsequent generations, through an absolute decrease in mortality and morbidity rates. In effect, at a later point in time, more children will survive to reproduce as a result of this "cleansing" process.

In contrast, an outbreeding population, by promoting heterozygosity, allows for the potentially dangerous recessive genes to remain extant, though dormant, in the gene pool. This prevails because, in this alternative, the recessive genes are more likely to be passed on to the next generation singularly, and thus harmlessly. On the other hand, the recessive genes and their negative consequences will sporadically appear over time with mating between unknown or distantly related individuals who share this characteristic. As a consequence, outbreeding may have a continuous slightly negative effect on population growth over the long term.[6]

Although it is difficult to substantiate this argument with reliable figures, some have suggested that for an expanding population outbreeding would actually increase the absolute number of deaths over the long term (Cavalli-Sforza and Bodmer 1971:765). Without denying either eventual effect on the population, others have noted that outbreeding is nonetheless biologically advantageous, as the dormant recessive genes, a portion of which are not deleterious, remain viable. This condition provides the population with greater evolutionary adaptability (Demarest 1977:337).

All of the above allows for the conclusion that inbreeding has immediate disadvantages for those most closely involved. However, this is probably not the case for a population if it is viewed as an evolutionary organism adapting to its ecological surroundings over time. The hidden agenda item which prompted this discussion of the effects of inbreeding is, not surprisingly, concerned with how this information has eventually influenced existing explanations for the "universality of the incest taboo." Some commentators have used the data or assumptions about it to support the contention that the effects prompted avoidance of the prohibition to take effect by focusing primarily on the immediate and obvious consequences of inbreeding. By considering the implications of inbreeding for a population, others noted above have argued just the opposite, since this factor cannot be shown to have a negative consequence.

Interpreting this latter demographic information more specifically, it has even been suggested that it is possible to catch a glimmer of the emergence of the incest prohibition at a specific point in human evolution and prehistory. Washburn and De Vore (1961: 99–100) cautiously suggest that the hunting-gathering lifestyle of primitive humanity during the Middle Pleistocene of a half-million years ago would have created favorable conditions for the emergence of an incest prohibition among family members through a recognition of the advantages of the exchange of offspring among neighboring groups. Ember (1983:101–102) also considers the matter of a time frame for the emergence of the prohibition, but opts for a much later period. He suggests the Neolithic era of ten thousand years ago, characterized by farming and herding, which resulted in human population growth and expansion, as an optimal point for tracing the emergence and effects of the prohibition.

In this context of historical and theoretical speculation the name, if not the visage, of the presumedly incestuous Cleopatra often makes its attractive appearance, to counter any claims about the negative significance of inbreeding on the emergence of the taboo. The welter of arguments often moves rashly from the general and abstract to the particular and concrete. Therefore it would be best to make explicit what has obviously been lurking behind this introduction to the consequences of incest by considering some of the more well-known explanations for either the prohibition or voluntary absence of incest in human societies. Their points of contention become quickly apparent, but their common unstated assumptions emerge only in due course. It no longer becomes an issue of determining the effects of incest, but rather how best to interpret these in the course of human affairs. This is a more delicate and nebulous concern, since it bears indirectly on the question of the definition of human nature and culture.

CHAPTER 3

The Culture
of the Solutions

The researches which we propose to make in the present
work led us into paths which have of late years been trod-
den by many men of more or less importance

STARCKE, 1888

THE EPIGRAPH SUGGESTS that a lengthy dissertation, rather than a
single chapter, could be orchestrated on the existing explanations
for the prohibition of incest. Apparently this topic was already well
worn by the late nineteenth century. However, this familiarity has
failed to dampen the enthusiasm of twentieth-century scholars, who
continue to seek meaning in the academic exercise. Moreover, there is
no reason to suspect that this familiar intellectual path alluded to
above will be abandoned in the future. In contrast, some of the
other ambitious questions posed by the forerunners of contemporary
social science have, for the most part, been dismissed as irrelevant
by a succeeding generation of thinkers. This sort of scholarly aban-
donment must strike those in other disciplines who build on solutions as a peculiar process of intellectual development, but it is
characteristic of social theory.

Intriguing questions about the genesis and diffusion of some item,
idea, custom, or institution were commonly the subject matter of
volumes. Today, if mentioned at all, these concerns are dispensed
with in a sentence or two as having been ill-conceived projects. The
advent of functionalism in social science during this century insti-
gated a concern for relationships of customary behaviors and the
useful contributions of customary behaviors, rather than the ori

gins. More recently, symbolic and structural interpretations have delved into the meaning of the same arrangements. In a word, the search for the origins of social behavior became unfashionable. Interestingly enough, this trend does not hold for the question of the source of the incest taboo. This enigma still commands inordinate attention, especially for anthropologists whose broad-based discipline emerged most intimately and comfortably associated with the search for human beginnings. Thus today the literature on this topic continues to display a rare, if not unique, multilayered theoretical character as some investigators continue to search for origins, others for functions, and still others for cultural meaning. In addition, the implications of psychology, ecology, ethology, demography, and biology are brought to bear in an often bewildering display of accumulated wisdom. Yet there is still no recognizable consensus, especially on the question of the origin of the incest prohibition.

In itself, such a situation has to be accounted for in some fashion. It is insufficient to suggest that the continued interest in this topic can be tied to the fact that there can be no saisfactory solution. Admittedly, and this is a crucial observation, there is no direct evidence on this subject, only deduction and speculation. This is likely to be the case always. However, there have been other questions of a similar nature, such as the original form of religion, or descent systems, especially whether matriarchy preceded patriarchy or vice versa, which cannot be directly answered, either. As noted, in the main these inquiries have now been deemed uninteresting or irrelevant. The inability to provide a verifiable thesis for the origin of the taboo is no doubt a compelling aspect of this intellectual complex. However, it is the fascination with the problem, rather than answers, which invites each generation of social theorists to demonstrate their intellectual wares and apply the latest sovereign remedy to an age-old problem.

Anthropologists themselves have long recognized the significance of isolating key concepts or thematic idioms in the study of other cultures. These are ideas central to a people's view and experience of its universe by imparting related meaning to other and sometimes seemingly disparate ideas and activities. In a more general sense, these key notions make a particular lifestyle worth pursuing by their pervasive meaning. In light of the history of the thinking on

the incest taboo, it seems reasonable to view this fascination for the subject as such a key concept, since its existence, implications, and interpretations give primary meaning to the anthropological exercise. Although not always stated, which is not unexpected when dealing with such profound ideas, the thinking on this subject is concerned with explicating what makes for humanity and society. On a more recognizable and practical level, the incest taboo is the collective anthropological stock in trade. At issue when the topic is taken under advisement is the nature of human nature and what anthropologists in particular have to offer in defining and interpreting it for others.

In light of what has gone before, in terms of the numerous critiques of one type of theory in favor of advancing another, considerable restraint will be exercised here in bringing together this material. This course is adopted not because what others have already written is uninteresting or erroneous so as to be casually dismissed. Many of these predecessors were great men, who earned their accolades from admiring colleagues and the literate public of their day. In addition, there were others, equally erudite in their thinking and production, who did and do not deserve their relative lack of fame. Oddly enough, many of these more obscure figures were much more cautious in their interpretations of the ethnographic data, and took up positions more in line with contemporary observations. Since they could not be as easily used as intellectual foils for those who came after and knew more, they earned obscurity, in contrast to their more often discounted colleagues.

Taken collectively, there is now little reason to consider in detail what they had to say on the origin of the incest taboo. Their thoughts have often been recounted by each other, and today in many other publications. However, in recalling their visions of an obscure past, I am more concerned with what might have made previous commentators take a certain position and the potential meaning they and their readers might have found in their words. Adopting this attitude permits a recognition and appreciation of a deep-seated agreement on profound issues about human nature. This tacit agreement was arrived at in spite of more apparent controversy. An element of contentiousness marked their own discussions in often lively fashion, and their differences continue to provide a means for classifying respective approaches to the problem. However, is it reasonable to conclude that articulate men of a particular place and time, with all this implies in terms of common cultural influences, will find only disagreement on a subject so profound as what makes for human nature? Moreover, in their time, as opposed to now, this issue often emerged as a factor in distinguishing civilized from potentially uncivilized behavior. The extent and complexities of prohibited sexual and marital arrangements among distant natives were not yet fully appreciated by these commentators, so far removed from their subjects in the capitals of Europe and America. In addition to superficial differences, the result was, not surprisingly, a profound but elusive agreement on the probable origin and evolution of the incest taboo.

In brief, the common cause was the unstated belief that humans were responsible for inventing the incest taboo, in recognition of its presumed or recognizable benefits. For these nineteenth-century theorists, as for many today, the incest prohibition defined humanity and cultured existence, so it was eminently reasonable to assume a priori that the species was somehow consciously and actively involved in its cultural evolution. To entertain an idea otherwise is to detract significantly from this exalted vision of humanity. Yet this agreeable vision is not the only way to view the issue.

Typical methods for absorbing the existing approaches to the problem have been to classify them as having either a sociological or biological basis. Alternatively, it is possible to judge them as to whether they provide an explanation, whatever its value, for the origin of the prohibition or sometimes, in unrecognized fashion, offer an account for its continued existence in terms of its contemporary function.[1] The origin and function explanations for the incest taboo are not necessarily the same thing, nor are they necessarily mutually exclusive in generating an understanding of human social behavior. However, in terms of the problem under consideration, it is best to recognize the differences involved and keep these separate for a time. Although there is some temporal overlap and the expected generational mavericks to contend with, an intellectual cycle has essentially run its course in just about a hundred years. Explicit pseudohistorical explanations for the emergence of the incest taboo were generally characteristic of nineteenth- and early

twentieth-century social thought. This approach was later sup-
planted by more sociological concerns with the function of the
taboo, which attempted to account for its persistence as the result
of its contribution to harmonious social relations. Recently there
has been a renewed interest in possible explanations for origins,
through the synthesis of data and perspectives from different academic fields.

Despite this smooth geometric image of the genesis and flow of
ideas, breaking into the circle of thought does some injustice to
intellectual history. For example, the functionalism of the mid-
twentieth century bore the definite imprint of early nineteenth-
century utilitarian thought on social issues, even on the particular
score of the prohibition of familiar sexuality. Thus Jeremy Bentham
wrote, almost two hundred years ago, that there were "inconveni-
ences" of incest which would include "Rivalry between house members" and "Relaxation of domestic discipline." He also added that
incest would be dangerous to the health of the young, as the result
of "premature indulgence," and the absence of the prohibition
would deprive a girl "of marriage and its advantages."[2] The latter
two suggestions may now seem a bit unfashionable, but the first two
ideas are dated only by expository style, since they are readily com-
prehensible in comparison to contemporary sociological discourse.
Even the eighteenth century had its functionalist, since Hoebel re-
minds us that Lord Henry St. John Bolingbroke (1678–1751) wrote
that the prohibition of incest served ". . . to improve sociability
among men and to extend it as wide as possible, in opposition to
that insociability which is apt to grow up between distinct families
and states" (quoted in Hoebel 1953:281).[3]

This prevailing concern with practicalities, however, was diminished by the mid-nineteenth century, when others concluded, on
the basis of the rapidly accumulating accounts of native peoples
of the world, that it might be possible to do more than comment on
the mundane prevailing implications of the incest taboo. It was
generally assumed at the time that such "primitive" groups displayed in their social organization, particularly in terms of marriage
and family relations, previous stages in the social history of our
kind. Thus it was believed that it might be possible to glimpse in
their contemporary midsts evidence for the emergence of the taboo

itself. This conclusion ushered in a lively controversy on the evolution of human societies. Although the problem was never resolved to their own complete satisfaction, nor even less to that of those who followed, this intellectual climate provides a convenient entry point to more recent thinking on the origin of the incest prohibition.

An exemplar is provided by the prodigious academic feats of the mid-nineteenth-century New York lawyer and passionate ethnographer Lewis Henry Morgan. In addition to his particular concern for recording the precontact culture of the Iroquois Indians, he developed a general interest in reconstructing the social evolution of humankind through his meticulous investigations into the then extant variety of family and marriage forms. Their extensions, which generate wider kinship systems and related terminologies, were also studied in detail. On the basis of this ethnographic data, which poured in from all over the world as the result of questionnaires he sent to resident Europeans with some knowledge of these affairs, he developed in *Ancient Society* (1877) an elaborate typology depicting the evolutionary stages of marriage and family as social institutions. An overriding assumption of the work was the belief that some societies, including our own, had progressed through earlier arrangements, while others still maintained their more primitive expression due to their lower position on the evolutionary scale. These remaining societies thus provided a living history of social forms which he believed could still be charted in the present.

As a careful interpreter of the information, he denied the existence of societies which still allowed for marriage between parents and offspring or siblings. Nonetheless, he argued it was still possible to discern a hint of this now extinct "consanguine family" by analyzing the kinship terms of the succeeding "punaluan family," which was extant among certain Polynesian groups. In this second of five stages in the evolution of the family, marriage between brother and sister was no longer permissible, but lingering kinship terms suggested this was once the case. For Morgan, the characteristic linguistic custom in these societies of a child referring to the father's sister by the same term he employed for the mother, and similarly calling mother's brother by the term used for father, implied that at a stage in the past, siblings had joined in approved marriages. These remaining kinship terms, as linguistic fossils, suggested to Morgan that at some point in human history a child's parents would also have been brother and sister to each other. It is now thought more reasonable to conclude that these very terms suggest that marriage could not take place between those who referred to each other as parent or child. This was and still is the custom in many societies. However, one cannot but admire Morgan's ingenuity in constructing a convoluted argument to support his evolutionary dogma.

In addition to arranging the hypothetical facts in temporal sequence, Morgan was also concerned with explanations for changing marriage forms. This change necessarily implied an account for the emergence of the taboo which, by his punaluan stage, had prohibited the marriage of close kin. For Morgan the explanation, though advanced tentatively and vaguely, was to be deduced as an aspect of evolutionary biology, since he interpreted the incest taboo as "a good illustration of natural selection at work" (1877:425). However, this was natural selection with a human component, since, rather than impersonal biological laws, it was instead the primitive intellect at work, for in due course the "evils" of sibling marriage would come under observation. Thus he wrote that this advance in human social forms ". . . . required the surrender of a privilege which savages would be slow to make. Commencing, it may be supposed, in isolated cases, with a slow recognition of its advantages, it remained an experiment through immense expanses of time, then becoming general . . ." (1877:425). Thus, for Morgan, it was the crucial intervention of human intelligence, rather than independent biological forces, which accounted for the purposeful elimination of primordial incestuous promiscuity and the emergence of the prohibition.[4]

Although the origin of the incest taboo was a relatively minor item on Morgan's ambitious agenda and a rationale for its existence merely alluded to, his name is usually linked, somewhat misleadingly, with a "biological" theory for its emergence. In point of fact, he was more inclined toward the cultural recognition of the biological implications of inbreeding, which is a very different matter. The typical reaction to Morgan's supposition has been to suggest that primitive humanity, in a state of biological ignorance, would be incapable of recognizing the potentially deleterious effects of inbreeding. This response was posed early on by the renowned Sir James Frazer, who argued vaguely, though apparently in more rigid biological fashion, that "blind savages blindly obeyed the impulse of great evolutionary forces . . ." (1910:169). Morgan's position continues to be dismissed today, on the grounds that there are no deleterious effects of inbreeding. However, as noted earlier, this reaction, often adopted by anthropologists, is an oversimplification and a potentially erroneous interpretation of the findings of genetics and medicine. In point of fact, close inbreeding is more likely than not to have immediate and recognizable physical effects on the offspring.

None of this would be admissible as evidence, however, if we consider the even more profound and intriguing question of whether or not our distant ancestors could reasonably have been aware of the actual relationship between sexual relations and reproduction itself. Upon reflection, this relationship is not obvious. One consequence does not necessarily follow from the other, and if it does, there is a rather lengthy interval between cause and effect. At the least, it has to be acknowledged that this information is not intuitive among humans. Even in societies such as our own, this literally vital information has to be passed on from one generation to another, in order to avoid social embarrassment. However, the reported existence of two societies in the Pacific whose members claim no such knowledge of the facts of life but do not engage in incest lends some controversial ethnographic support to the idea that biological consequences in the form of reproduction should not be considered a relevant factor in the emergence of the prohibition. Whatever value such an objection can have is difficult to estimate, in light of the near universality of the contrary situation and in consideration of the suggestion that these few exceptional societies may be expressing their biological insights metaphorically.[5] On the other hand, it is equally difficult to be assured of the supposition that negative consequences originally stimulated a prohibition on inbreeding, even though this may be the case. There are many instances in the ethnographic record of societies which espouse this opinion (see Burton 1973), but then there are others which take no apparent interest in this matter. The issue is moot and not resolvable by reference to extant cultures.

The familiar aphorism "Marry out or be killed out," coined in 1889 by Edward Tylor, one of the first academic anthropologists, provides an alternate view of the matter, since it points to the potential social, rather than biological, advantages of prohibiting marriage between members of the nuclear family. Although unrecognized at the time, Taylor's proposition restated the problem by shifting attention away from a concern with an explanation for the barrier against sex and reproduction within the family to a consideration of why marriage takes place outside of it. As noted, from an abstract perspective, sex and marriage are quite separate matters; and they are not mutually exclusive, since a hypothetical society could allow sex within the nuclear family but also prohibit marriage among its members (Fox 1983:54–55).[6] In effect, the rule prohibiting sex among family members is different from the one which enforces marriage outside of it. On the other hand, such a distinction between sex and marriage was not recognized by Victorian sensibilities, which joined the two in idealized fashion. Therefore, it is reasonable to assume that Tylor and others who adopted this vision of the problem, and its subsequent resolution, thought they were explaining the prohibition against incestuous sex. Their remarks provide an insight into their world view that is of equal concern as their misguided explanations for the prohibition against incest.

There is also the question of whether this sort of argument, which alludes to the potential dire consequences of restricting social contacts, in contrast to the assumed favorable consequences of external marital alliances, is concerned with origins or functions in the sense of how exogamy contributes to societal solidarity. Again, these may be separate matters, since the existing prohibition on sex within the family, in conjunction with prescribing marriage outside of it, may have come into existence for one reason and then conferred secondary social advantages which follow from the arrangement. Therefore, recognizing the latter functional contributions does not imply a solution to the initial problem of the origination of a custom. These complexities may now be apparent, but this was not the case for Tylor, since he assumed that his marrying-out adage was an explanation for the origin of the incest prohibition, rather than a function of its persistence. Recalling that he also took no explicit cognizance of a distinction between sex and marriage, his intent was clear from his words: "Again and again in the world's history, savage tribes must have had plainly before their minds the simple practical alternative between marrying-out or being killed-out" (Tylor 1889:267). These lines suggest that Tylor was of the opinion that human beings consciously promulgated an incest prohibition in order to take advantage of the favorable social consequences this entailed. In contrast to Morgan, Tylor was obviously more sociologically inclined, and assumed our primitive ancestors were of a similar bent. Yet it must be noted that they both gave credit to human consciousness for the institutionalization of initial sexual and marriage prohibitions while merely disagreeing on the motivation for such arrangements.

For the sake of completeness, it should be noted that the usual objection to Tylor's line of reasoning draws attention to the alternative view that marital alliances may not necessarily confer peaceful political cooperation among different groups. The many societies espousing the statement "We marry our enemies" could offer plausible support for either position, depending upon how this maxim is interpreted. It might imply that marriage with allies could threaten an existing peaceful coalition or, alternatively, that such arrangements are thought to mitigate disharmonious ones. A more familiar contrary example, provided this time by Queen Victoria rather than Cleopatra, suggests that, although her daughters were married to many other European rulers, this failed to prevent a world war in the succeeding generation by opposed states headed by first cousins. Such conflicting examples as these do little more than note that the potential advantages of marital alliance are not always realized, in contrast to those who have adopted this conclusion as self-evident. However, neither position offers direct evidence for the emergence of the incest prohibition or rules of exogamy, since their concern is with potential contemporary results of such arrangements which are then projected on the past.

Although this would not exhaust the list of candidates from the last century who took up the challenge, the name of the Scottish lawyer John McLennan surely deserves an honorable mention. His *Primitive Marriage*, which first appeared in 1865, introduced the concepts of exogamy and endogamy (in refreshing fashion, he apologized for these neologisms in a footnote), and thus the systematic concern for the origin of marriage regulations. His study, however, was more influential as the consequence of his admirable comparative analysis of kinship and marriage systems. Less memorable, though, was his concern for "bride capture" and his interpretations of this presumed practice, which were more closely allied to his vague comments on the incest prohibition. Specifically, and not without some originality of thought, McLennan attempted a dubious symbolic interpretation of the circumstances and ideas among primitive peoples, past and present, which produced "a system of capturing the women of foreign tribes for wives" (1970:12). Although this custom was no longer extant, McLennan believed it could be deduced from some examples provided by antiquarian literary sources and the behavior of existing "rude tribes" which symbolized forcible capture of the bride at their marriage ceremonies. For McLennan, this peculiar practice was best interpreted as a ritual residue of a previous, unrecorded stage when the seizure of women was an actual fact. He supposed this was due to their relative scarcity as the outcome of female infanticide. Once set in motion, this scramble for a foreign bride, even where and when no longer necessary, had established the practice of exogamy among primitive peoples. To do otherwise, even when possible, would be so irregular as to be considered unacceptable (1970:114–115). This reference to the emergence of common sentiments and reliance on the unstated idea that "custom is king" to account for a practice is obviously weak and tautological, but apparently the best McLennan could offer in explanation for the other social arrangements he analyzed with such perspicacity. Furthermore, his theory of bride capture was also aimed at an explication of the custom of marrying out, rather than the prohibition of incest, which, as previously mentioned, was a common and understandable synthesis of ideas for the time.

The preceding few pages, devoted to the thoughts of some intellectual ancestors, obviously do not do justice to the scope of their investigations and overall accomplishments. However, in contrast to the impression conveyed by most contemporary reviews of the literature, the foregoing, attenuated as it may be, is an adequate proportional representation of these nineteenth-century predecessors' attention to the opaque question of the origin of incest prohibitions vis-à-vis their more acute concern for the rules of exogamy. The unintentional image projected today by those with an interest in incest prohibitions is that many of these illustrious forefathers had an equal fascination with this problem, and had rendered some dogmatic and systematic assertions on these matters. An actual consideration of their work as a whole indicates quite clearly that this was not the case on either score. Incest prohibitions or marriage rules, as questions of origin, were of relatively little concern to them. Moreover, their explanations for these customs were little more than haphazard and equivocal asides. Their fascination, indeed their obsession, was with a presumed previous stage in human history, thought to be characterized by unbridled sexual behavior. This was a more attractive, and presumably more rewarding, fixation for Victorian imaginations than what they had to contend with in their present.

On the potential origin of rules of exogamy and, by his implication, of incest prohibitions, McLennan summed up in his concluding chapter: ". . . it will be remarked that we have not spent time on a consideration of the question . . ." (1970:114). In a similar vein, on the same subjects, Tylor simply stated: ". . . no observer has ever seen it come into existence, nor have the precise conditions of its origins yet been clearly inferred" (1889:267). Finally, as already mentioned, Morgan merely suggested, in vague fashion, that an inevitable recognition of the biological consequences of inbreeding eventually resulted in its prohibition (1877:425), and Frazer briefly alluded to some "blind impulses" which had the same result (1910:169). As suggested, this brevity of interest and the unrefined formulations are not conveyed by contemporary reviews of this topic, which present an overly systematic reordering of past "theories" and "theorists." The word "theory" is usually loosely applied in social science, but even with such an exigency to promote some random ideas to a higher intellectual plane, it is hardly a realistic appraisal to imply that any of those just cited had a theory about the origin of the incest taboo.

In addition to an intellectual inflation, this characterization deflects attention away from the matter of their greater concern, which involved more industry in reconstructing an unobservable past, where limitations on sexual and marital behavior did not prevail. These scenarios, depicting primitive promiscuity, incestuous unions, group marriage, primal hordes, and the like at some obscure point in the past of all humanity, and still vaguely perceptible among the "lower races," were clearly the greater concern of nine-teenth-century interpreters of history and customs. These hypo-thetical situations not only provided a necessary baseline for truly elaborate theories of social evolution, but also suited the fancy of Victorian thought. Thus Lubbock, one of the popularizers of this genre, warned his readers at the outset that he was not always able to spare them from some "repugnant" details on the sexual and marital customs among "modern savages" (1978:lxvi). Although not quite as erudite and original a thinker as many of his contem-poraries, Lubbock does provide a clearer expression of their consen-sus in his publication for a more general audience.

Without denigrating their many other accomplishments, it must nonetheless be recognized that, in generating unrecorded scenes of primitive promiscuity, these authors were forced to rely on either imagination or complicated interpretations of existing marriage customs in other cultures to buttress their contentions. With the advantages of hindsight and more reliable information gathered later by actual fieldworkers, it is not difficult now to recognize the intellectual foibles of recent anthropological forerunners. In con-sidering their general pronouncements about the primeval state of human nature, one now suspects them of repairing to their studies and conjuring up wistful images of both past and distant societies. These primal scenes served, in part, to afford an attractive antithesis of ideal Victorian social arrangements, rather than verifiable propo-sitions. Without denying the rational need for a primitive social stage of human evolution, it is also possible to explain their fascina-tion for, and proclivity to construct, imaginary social systems that bore little resemblance to the facts and merely satisfied a need for cultural oppositions. These imagined alternatives from distant times and places imparted positive meaning to the relatively enviable condition of nineteenth-century advancement and may even have provided intellectual relief from the more oppressive norms of the day.[7] The fact that these fabricated societies did not have an his-torical or ethnographic base was irrelevant. What was of relevance was the fact that total sexual freedom, especially in the form of what would have been deemed incestuous sex or marriage, was no longer directly recognizable among human populations in the last century.

As a result of this line of reasoning, these writers were forced to admit to the emergence of the incest taboo at some point in time. However, as suggested, this was a minor by-product of their often more elaborate commentaries about a previous stage when it was absent. This explains their attenuated and casual remarks on this intrusive custom. Adopting a temporal view of primal promiscuity demanded, with no outward deliberation, that the incest prohibition was a human invention, since it was preceded by total sexual freedom. Thus a basic standard of what was taken for granted as cultural behavior was in itself a product of culture. This was agreed upon without debate.

The significance of the element-of sexual promiscuity in the past provides a partial explanation for the popularity of Morgan, McLennan, Tylor, and Frazer in their time, and their continued influence in the present, in comparison to equally learned commentators on primitive societies, such as Wake, Starcke, Kohler, Crawley, Letourneau, Robertson Smith, and Westermarck. The latter list includes scholars more or less similarly inclined toward an evolutionary perspective, but who took a position in direct contradiction to the then more fashionable and attractive idea of primitive sexual promiscuity. In some cases, as with Westermarck, this was prompted by a theoretical disagreement, to be considered later. However, for the others, their opposition could be laid to more cautious and intellectually rigorous interpretations of the ethnographic facts at hand during the era.[8] For example, in 1889, Wake totally rejected the idea that evidence could exist to allow for the belief in a past primal horde characterized by sexual freedom (1967:13, 53). At the same time, in addition to marking the contrast between sex and marriage which escaped his contemporaries, Starcke also took general objection to the image of primitive promiscuity (1976). Writing a few years later, a similar contentious example is offered by Crawley, who admirably suggested in all simplicity: "It is unscientific to have recourse to a hypothesis of primitive incest and promiscuity" (1960, Vol. II:205).

Even more interesting, in considering the relative lack of contemporary fame of these figures, is that their partial refusal to admit to hypothetical stages and ancient customary survivals was more in harmony with the ideas of a successive generation of fieldworker anthropologists who explicitly debunked such tableaux as "just-so" stories. Yet the authors of these pronounced fictions remained paramount in anthropological discussions, because they provided excellent intellectual foils to those who came after.[9] This suggests that it assures more fame to be deemed wrong at the right time than right at the wrong time, as far as the collective memory of scholarship is concerned.

Although there are vast differences on other scores, in terms of the specific problem of the incest prohibition, Freud provides the most illustrious example of an individual being judged generally incorrect by contemporary anthropology, yet failing to suffer from the expected consequences. Freud's case is a complex one, since his ideas about infantile sexuality and the Oedipal complex were not denied, but rather considered to be beyond the scope of social anthropology which, following Durkheim, sought the definition of and solution to sociological, rather than psychological, problems. In addition, Freud's interpretation of the form of the Oedipal complex was seriously challenged early on by Malinowski (1927 and 1929), on the grounds of cultural variations in attitudes toward sex, as well as in light of varying family and descent forms. Malinowski arrived at this conclusion on the basis of the ethnographic data collected among the Trobriand Islanders, who traced descent matrilineally. Thus they vest formal jural authority over a boy in the hands of his mother's brother, rather than his father. As a consequence, Malinowski argued, this maternal uncle became the object of unconscious homicidal desires, while the sister, who is expressly forbidden to him as a sexual partner, became the object of a boy's incestuous wishes. Moreover, this repression took place at a later stage in the psychosexual development of the male child, since his early years were marked by adult indifference to sexual displays with those around him. Thus, in an early and single ethnographic stroke, Malinowski both accepted and rejected Freud's insights on childhood sexuality and the universality of the Oedipal complex. Although recently challenged by Spiro with specific reference to the Trobriand data (1982), Malinowski's revision of

Freud's unconscious model became accepted dogma in the social sciences and even grudgingly admitted to by psychoanalysis.[10]

Whether or not the Oedipal complex is universal in form or forms has been a constant issue taken up in textbooks and academic monographs. However, more controversial questions about the reality of Freud's vision, derived from his failure to acknowledge incest itself, have received more recent popular exposure in books, newspaper, and magazine articles.[11] The issue here is not the male child's repressed sexual desire for his mother, but the obverse: the father's sexual interest in his daughter. For psychoanalytic dogma, the failure to resolve satisfactorily the first leads to personality disorders, while, according to social workers, the second may lead to physical manifestations and a now recognized social problem of debated proportions. In essence, contemporary critics have suggested that, for whatever conscious or unconscious reason, Freud engaged in either a cover-up or denial of actual incest between father and daughter in the process of promulgating his theory of incest fantasy as the etiology of female neurosis.

His detractors universally point out that in 1892, in collaboration with Breuer, the young Freud indicated the significance of childhood sexual trauma on adult cases of female "hysteria" (Breuer and Freud 1955). Some years later, in an appended footnote to a reissue of another early paper espousing this view, Freud recanted: "This section is dominated by an error which I have repeatedly acknowledged and corrected. At that time I was not yet able to distinguish between my patients' fantasies about their childhood years and their real recollections. As the result I attributed to the aetiological factor of seduction a significance and universality which it does not possess" (Freud 1955:168).

The implications of this footnote, which now assume epical proportions, were first noted in recent times in a relatively obscure publication by Peters (1976), a practicing psychoanalyst in a counseling clinic, where he dealt with confirmed incest cases on a regular basis. In his reconsideration of psychoanalytic orthodoxy, Peters also notes that in 1925 Freud admitted to suppressing the information that in two published cases of female hysteria, the fathers had indeed "molested" their daughters (Freud 1955:203). In passing, Peters also mentions that many of Freud's teachers, colleagues, and even patients took strong objection with his initial diagnosis on the origin of female hysteria (1976:399). Peters concludes that, as a result of both cultural and personal factors, Freud became genuinely more inclined toward the fantasy notion of incest. On the one hand, it relieved the collective conscience of adults and, more important, it led to his recognition of unconscious childhood sexuality and its role in personality formation.[12] In a word, Freud "oversubscribed" to the fantasy theory (Peters 1976:401).

Other, more recent commentators have not been as kind to the father figure of psychoanalysis in more public forums. Some have referred to the inevitable "bankruptcy" of psychoanalytic theory as the result of Freud's failure to confront reality.[13] Recognizing the implications of his influential conclusion to the definition and treatment of women in Western culture has led one commentator to declare Freud's view an unintentional cover-up of the sexual abuse of young girls (Rush 1980:83). Another interprets both incest and Freud's theoretical avoidance of it as integral and inevitable features of the oppressive nature of our "patriarchal" family system (Herman 1981:9). The rhetoric in these instances is passionate. Despite this tone, a spirit of objectivity requires the recognition of Freud's shortsightedness and even obfuscation on this particular issue in the context of his otherwise revolutionary view of human nature. The inability to confront the actual incestuous deed by adults, as opposed to the unconscious desire to fulfill it by children, also had an impact on Freud's explanation of the origin of the prohibition. In effect, incest for Freud was moralized out of existence with the promulgation of the taboo, but not before some memorable deeds by borderline humanity.

Freud's exposition of the historical events is contained in *Totem and Taboo*, which first appeared in German in 1913 during the reign of evolutionary anthropology. The essay contains all the intellectual hallmarks of the era and, befitting its authorship by the founder of a new discipline, it also interjects some noteworthy additions to the prevailing world view. The emerging generation of anthropologists, however, were not very impressed by the old and new Freud offered in his treatise on the origin of the prohibition. Rieff remarks that *Totem and Taboo* became " 'ritual fare' for the anthropologists and other social scientists, an occasion for the methodological slaying of the great father" (1961:249). Although the reaction was more akin to the ritual response to an interloping patriarch from another academic primal horde, the end result was the same, rejection.[14]

Following the great anthropologists such as Frazer, Freud relied upon an evolutionary interpretation of social behavior in other cultures and accepted the idea, as was common for the day, that the Australian Aborigines were the closest living examples of the earliest stage of human history. He assumed that, while more inclined to it, they also had a "horror" of incest, which was avoided by complex totemic kinship and marriage systems. In addition to the prevailing equation between primitives and Western children, Freud also suggested that their horror of incest ". . . reveals a striking agreement with the mental life of neurotic patients" (1950:17), since it took on an obsessional form.

Here again it has to be remembered that Freud was confusing sex with marriage regulations. Therefore, these exogamic marriage systems were no indication that the Aborigines had a horror of incest, and even less that they were obsessed by the subject. The fixation, if anyone's, was Freud's, since he grappled with the implications of incest for most of his intellectual life. Although Freud was misguided by the work of others in concluding that totemism was a total religious system, he was original in suggesting a relationship between religious ideas and neurosis. Although others may have considered it a further offense, in Freud's defense it should be mentioned that he was making no invidious distinction between primitive and contemporary religious practices, since he viewed all as a form of obsessional neuroses.

Relying upon the ideas of Frazer, Darwin, and the Semitic scholar Robertson Smith, Freud suggested that the original patriarchal horde of primal social organization was shattered when the sons banded together in opposition to the father, who monopolized the women of the group. After killing him, "Cannibal savages as they were, it goes without saying that they devoured their victim as well . . ." (Freud 1950:142). Subsequently overcome by guilt, they rejected their sisters as well as their own daughters as sexual partners and sought women elsewhere. Thus, as Freud writes: "The dead father became stronger than the living one . . ." (1950:143), for his murder and consumption were ironically the last precultural human deeds. This was Freud's startling conclusion, for he argued that the emotional response set in motion the beginnings of social organization with the emergence of the incest prohibition, moral restrictions on behavior, and religion in the form of totemism.

Despite the now prominent nature of these remarks, the actual scenario was presented in a few sentences and its "exactitude" and "certainty" immediately qualified in a much longer footnote (Freud 1950:142–143). Whatever other value it may now have, this aside could hardly be labelled as a theory for the origin of the incest taboo. Freud's ideas could also be summed up as merely a series of assumptions about the inclination of humans to commit incest and the conscious promulgation of a prohibition against it under imagined conditions at some point in human history. For Freud, a distinction was his conclusion that this moral injunction marked the initial point of human consciousness.

This last remark draws attention to an ideational parallel between Freud and the equally celebrated Lévi-Strauss of contemporary social science. This link between past and present, however, is not tenuous, since the reigning master of social science reflects a definite Victorian outlook in his mode of scholarly inquiry. His multivolumed endeavors such as *Mythologiques*, his proclivity for roaming over the ethnographic landscape in single bounds in search of supportive evidence, and his concern for origins and laws governing human thought and behavior mark his genius and creative style. These trademarks set him off from contemporary anthropology to the extent that a confrontation with his ideas is simultaneously an intellectual journey into the past, present, and future of humanity. A complete immersion into his sea of ideas can be unsettling, but the aim here is fortunately more limited. His thoughts on the origin of the incest prohibition, although not a simple matter, are the main concern.

At the very beginning of his discussion of the problem in *The Elementary Structures of Kinship*, Lévi-Strauss enigmatically states that the prohibition of incest is at once "social and pre-social" and that this ambiguity accounts for the "sacredness" of the rule (1969:12). For Lévi-Strauss, this equivocal status of the phenomenon is its defining feature, so that any attempt to explain the prohibition by reducing it to the realm of either nature or culture has been doomed to failure from the very outset. This definition of the situation allows him to consider and immediately reject existing theories which recognized only the biological or social implications of the prohibition. For Lévi-Strauss, befitting the nature of the topic, the existing explanations are themselves enveloped by "the aura of magical fear" (1969:10). He argues that the incest taboo touches on human sexual nature while at the same time existing as a social fact. Thus it is necessary to recognize the prohibition as a dynamic synthesis. Neither a feature of nature or culture, nor a composite of the two, the prohibition ". . . is the fundamental step because of which, by which, but above all in which, the transition from nature to culture is accomplished" (1969:24).

In effect, as with Freud, Lévi-Strauss views the prohibition of incest as the capacity which sets in motion social and cultural systems. Although the prohibition may be neither nature nor culture, it can concomitantly set humanity off from the animal world, which lacks this combining capacity. Subsequent developments in the study of animal societies since the publication of the book in 1949 and, more significant, his reliance on the even then outdated notions of genetics, forced Lévi-Strauss to reconsider these and other topics in the reissue of the English edition twenty years later. On the possibility of a finer line separating human and animal societies, Lévi-Strauss was admirably reflective and conciliatory. However, he refused to alter his rejection of any argument which suggested the significance of genetic effects on offspring was a conscious factor in promoting the prohibition. Presumably harking back to his original statement that such a position would imply "eugenic second-sight" (1969:13) for primitive society, he continued to reject this and other lines of reasoning (1969:xxix).

For his own part, Lévi-Strauss was inclined to accept an updated version of Tylor's earlier thesis about the social advantages of marital alliances and the renunciation of sexual privilege within the family.[15] In keeping with his theme of the fusion of nature and culture, Lévi-Strauss cites early studies of animals, albeit in controlled environments, which exhibit cooperative behavior of this sort as support for his alliance argument. Thus for Lévi-Strauss little abstract reasoning power is required by primal humans in order to recognize the advantages of sharing and exchange. This eventuality would instead be a "spontaneous resolution" of the problems of collective life (1969:42). Despite his deemphasis of the need for primate reasoning power, Lévi-Strauss nonetheless allows for the conscious recognition of the advantages of "marrying out" as a self-evident proposition. The incest prohibition may be attending to nature, but it is still a human convention. Lévi-Strauss sees in it, as did Tylor before him, the explanation for marriage rules.

Lévi-Strauss differs from previous commentators, however, by first offering an extensive and systematic consideration of his predecessors' ideas; and, by readvancing in more dogmatic fashion a previous explanation for the origin of the prohibition. In the process, he was among the first to create the impression of the existence of well-thought-out competing theories and schools of thought, which belies the rather halfhearted and scattered suggestions of others on this vexatious problem. Furthermore, although Lévi-Strauss identifies much of the previous thinking as magical, his own view of what is at issue is hardly straightforward or scientific in the sense of being verifiable. His characterization of the eventual evolution of presocial into social humanity is reminiscent of de Chardin's mystical rendition of human physical evolution, in which at some point the Creator breathes a soul into a brutish creature, with a simultaneous disturbance of "all spheres of life" (1965:163). For Lévi-Strauss, the collective soul of the species, the breath of sentient life as it were, is culture in sudden form by the abrupt appearance of the incest prohibition.

Lévi-Strauss's speculations on the origin and significance of the incest taboo and rules of exogamy, between which he failed to distinguish, provide a convenient terminus in this review of some of the ideas which surfaced and resurfaced in the past and present centuries in the anthropological search for human origins. This exercise was not undertaken in order to point to the deficits of existing theories, or to conclude in typical fashion that this legion of conflicting "just-so" stories fails to satisfy our curiosity on this subject. The individuals considered ever so briefly were men of intellectual substance who tempered the images of their and our times. The idea that the obvious flaws in their thinking could be quickly noted and rejected by any contemporary author suggests there is a problem, rather than a resolution to one. The facile treatment of our predecessors' "theories" is possible because, with the possible exception of Lévi-Strauss, they proposed no theories as such. Admittedly, they advanced a suggestion on the subject in the course of their investigations, but it would be hard to imagine that they were not as aware of its unsatisfactory nature as is today's typical undergraduate.

It has been suggested instead that their comments on this topic were compulsory ones as they sought the answer to other questions where their contributions are not as easily dismissed. Moreover, characterizing their insights as ones that often cancelled out each other fails to allow for an appreciation of their common intellectual ground. The link was their unstated assumption that, for some recognized reason or another, humanity instituted a prohibition on sex and reproduction among members of the nuclear family. This was to them self-evident. Their failure to consider otherwise is particularly surprising in light of the popularity of Darwinian notions which were making an otherwise profound impact on their times. The natural-selection hypothesis was only admitted to in the form of social Darwinism, which suggested that those primitive groups which recognized the value of marriage alliances would have social evolutionary advantages in the struggle for survival over those who did not. Darwin's more specific comments on the improbability of promiscuous intercourse in the state of nature generally went unheeded (1981:362) with the assumption that culture ushered in outbreeding among humans.

In fact, the intellectual trend was in the opposite direction, since Darwin fell under the influence of the social evolutionists in his thinking about human prehistory and progress. Although cautious on the quality of their evidence, Darwin felt compelled to defer to the authority of Lubbock, McLennan, and Morgan on primitive promiscuity, group marriage, and even the precedence of matrilineal over patrilineal descent in social evolution. However, Darwin adopted his position not without some perplexity and vacillation, since he concluded his remarks on this subject with the statement that he would not be willing to conjecture whether humans evolved from lower forms with "marriage" of some type or returned to such an arrangement after an intervening period of promiscuity (1981:

363). Thus, despite all the evidence from the animal world which Darwin had accumulated to advance the notion of the biological value of outbreeding, he was still unable to contemplate deleting the incest taboo from the human cultural inventory. This is not to suggest that he would have been correct in advancing such a line of reasoning, but it is surprising he did not entertain such a possibility. Others who came after have not been so reticent about turning to the animal kingdom in support of their theories, and have invoked Darwin's hallowed name in their cause. These new pioneers in the search for origins were preceded by a cohort of social scientists, primarily sociologists, who sought the contributions the incest taboo made to an orderly social life. Though their concerns were obviously different, they in no way altered prevailing assumptions.

CHAPTER 4

The Sociology
of the Problem

The family is an *organized* group [italics in original]

DAVIS, 1965

FOR THE NEXT generation of commentators in the mid-twentieth century, a curiosity about the prohibition of incest remained intact. However, their remarks reflect a dampened enthusiasm for the search for origins, which were deemed beyond recovery. They turned away from the past, to a consideration of the presumed contemporary functions of the incest prohibition. The intent was to determine the relationship of this sexual arrangement to other customs and its contribution to an orderly society. The implications of the difference between the origins as opposed to the functions of the rule were sometimes only implicit in their work, for they did not always make it clear that the perceived advantages they enumerated may have had little or nothing to do with the reason for the original appearance of the prohibition. In this respect, there was little to distinguish them from earlier thinkers, who had also concluded that the obvious social rewards of the denial of incest would be sufficient cause for the establishment of the prohibition. Thus it is not always reasonable to separate the two generations on the basis of the eventual conclusions drawn, since their initial premises were often similar. What does mark off the next generation, though, is the way in which it stated the problem. Twentieth-century social theory attacked the issue directly and specifically, as opposed to haphazardly musing on the prohibition as the consequence of a fixation on an even earlier stage of social life. In addition, these functionalists presumed that, since their temporal frame was the present, their propositions were verifiable, if not systematic, statements of a self-evident nature, rather than conjecture. However, their failure to consider incest and its consequences, which were possibilities to be reckoned with, led them to equally nebulous conclusions about the function of the prohibition as those of the predecessors.

Although the functionalist brand is usually applied to mid-century sociology, it makes more sense to initiate the discussion with Malinowski, a forerunner of British social anthropology, who drifted into the discipline, having already taken a doctorate in physics in Poland before deciding to go to England to study with Frazer. Malinowski's name is often associated with initiating the fieldwork tradition in anthropology, as the result of his extended stay on the Trobriand Islands during the First World War. His long-term residence among these people inclined him toward an appreciation of the interrelatedness of their particular social arrangements and customs. This concern placed him in opposition to the grander questions and universal scope of his teacher, for Frazer and his generation had no such concrete acquaintance with the perplexities of another culture. Nonetheless, Malinowski's more general view of human nature was tempered by this Trobriand interlude, as already noted by his reaction to the Freudian supposition of the universality of the Oedipal complex.

In the context of his running dispute with Freud's ideas and their active defense by Ernest Jones, Malinowski evolved his own views on the functional nature of the incest taboo. He was not totally unsympathetic to psychoanalysis, and as a perverse indication took some rhetorical delight in alluding to the potential unconscious significance of Freud's consistent misspelling of his critic Kroeber's name in publications (1927:172).[1] In a more serious and cooperative vein, Malinowski adopted some basic psychoanalytic propositions with the previously mentioned reservations he maintained about their specific universal form. However, as an insistent recorder of behavior and customs, Malinowski, the prototypical fieldworker, was uncompromisingly scornful of Freud's patricidal primal scene. He could not imagine how this fantastic tragedy of Freud's could be verified or have resulted in a universal rule. To

Malinowski, this was conjectural history of the worst kind. His response was to dispense with scenarios and temporal sequences altogether, by focusing on static relationships among social arrangements, such as the incest prohibition and the nuclear family.[2]

For Malinowski the human family evolved from early animal forms of social organization, though clearly distinguished from it by mating patterns and, equally important, by the human capacity for sentiment and culture, as opposed to instinct. The continued sexual receptivity of the human female and equally constant interest in her by the male, in conjunction with the long gestation period and dependency of the child, were the characteristic biological foundations of the human family. In addition, for Malinowski the human intellect provided the ability to recognize and continue to invest emotional interest in these relationships long after they served their biological functions. This implied the recognition of extended kinship bonds or society on a larger scale, which Malinowski believed was not found in the state of nature.

To this point, Malinowski's ideas are hardly distinguishable from early evolutionists, who viewed the family as the original human group from which society emerges, nor is his argument alien to the suppositions of contemporary neo-evolutionists, with their greater fixation on biological factors in the emergence of society. Where Malinowski distinguished himself was with the suggestion that the socialization of the child would be rendered more difficult, if not impossible, by sexual activity between parents and children. Incest therefore would be organizationally dysfunctional. Thus the prohibition and the family are coterminous, rather than one having precedence over the other. In terms of this line of reasoning, society could not exist otherwise. The presence of the incest prohibition, to Malinowski, was consistent with the existence of culture and social organization, which depended on the family as their source. The alternative, Malinowski suggested, would result in "the upsetting of age distinctions, the mixing up of generations, the disorganization of sentiments, and a violent exchange of roles . . ." (1927:251). The incest prohibition implied society in the sense of order, and incest implied the opposite, chaos. In less dramatic terms, for Malinowski the incest prohibition was a functional prerequisite of society.

Malinowski was, as mentioned, not the first to adopt this func tional and essentially synchronic interpretation of the rule prohibiting intrafamiliar sex, but he did advance the orientation in systematic fashion, in order to combat explicitly both psychological and pseudohistorical interpretations, which were very much the order of the day. In the process, the entire inquiry was radically altered without recognition from one concerned with primal sexuality, which implied incest, to a primal law, which entailed a lack of incest. Immorality was out and morality was in, as incest was transformed from a Victorian fantasy to a contemporary nonentity.

Taking Malinowski's lead, a subsequent generation of field anthropologists, employing their rapidly accumulating data, continued to display an interest in the functions of the prohibition, especially in the ethnographic context of varying marriage and descent systems. Their concern with rules of exogamy, which reflected such a wide variety of possibilities, even to the existence of societies which encouraged certain types of cousin marriage expressly forbidden in others, led them to take a dim view of any instinctual or biological explanation for incest prohibitions (see Murdock 1965). Whatever the substance or lack of value of previous attempts, the structuralfunctional critiques were partially misdirected in that they debunked previous explanations for the prohibition on familial sex by reference to new data on extensions. These social elaborations may well have different explanations and, more important, such evaluations switched the topic to a consideration of marriage regulations, which are quite different. To a great extent, the intellectual complex became more muddled than clarified with the influx of information on customs in other societies.

Sociologists, on the other hand, primarily restricted their inquiries to the Western family form and elaborated on the functional contributions of the incest taboo in a more abstract mode, since it was assumed the ethnographic context was well understood. Their contributions reemphasized the objective, positive effects of the incest taboo on social organization, but, possibly because our society was at issue, the formulations also began to take on subjective overtones not always recognizable in anthropological discourse. Dire consequences of all sorts were hinted at if the incest taboo were violated. These injunctions were of course issued in sometimes mystifying verbiage, but that is often the case with disguised ethical and moral pronouncements. Thus Talcott Parsons, one of America's most distinguished sociologists, wrote: ". . . on the societal level incest must be regarded as a regressive phenomenon, a withdrawal from the functions and responsibilities on the performance and fulfillment of which the transfamilial structures of society rest" (1954: 114). It is difficult to argue with such a supposition, for many reasons. The suggestion that society as we know it depends upon its present arrangements is a self-evident proposition. However, the characterization of incest as a potential threat to the social order deserves some verification.

Kingsley Davis, a similarly inclined functionalist, comes clean, as it were, in his introductory sociology text, where he metaphorically characterizes incest as a potentially "cancerous growth" within the nuclear family (1965:403). In explanation, Davis opts for the horror of confusion to account for the incest taboo's persistence. He argues that sex within the nuclear family, across the generations or even between them, would not only produce destructive domestic rivalry, but if reproduction were to take place, "the confusion of statuses would be phenomenal" (1965:402). By way of explication, he suggests that the male child of father-daughter incest ". . . would be brother of his own mother, i.e. the son of his own sister; a stepson of his own grandmother, possibly a brother of his own uncle; and certainly a grandson of his own father" (1965:403). Put this way, it certainly sounds too horrifying to contemplate. Whether or not the actual results would be equally confusing is a different matter. Although not an exact parallel, it is worth remembering that in the course of normal social life, everyone makes extensive status shifts, even in the context of kinship arrangements. The average male is both father and son, uncle and nephew, brother and cousin at the same time, and undergoes other redefinitions with time. Admittedly, this process may not be the same as the potential result of familial incest, but it provides some indication of the ability of humans to juggle their statuses without psychological collapse. Reproductive incest would require some further complexity, but more likely the social implications would be merely ignored for those involved. Not everyone is a sociologist, nor does everyone have the responsibility to project a uniform vision of the structure of the

Western family. However, those who do have this mandate might find their chore more complicated by the existence of incest and its admittedly confusing consequences. Incest might be a personal nightmare for those involved, but it also appears to strike some conceptual horror into sociologists concerned with the structure and function of the nuclear family.

This is not meant to suggest that contemporary sociologists are totally misguided in their statements about the persistent functions of the incest prohibition. These were enumerated some time ago in simple and abbreviated fashion by Malinowski, and they are not objectionable, in the main. There is a recognizable tautology involved, in the sense that the organization of the family, as it now exists, could not continue in this form if its present arrangements did not also hold constant. Specifically, the family and its present arrangements are the same thing. Moreover, as noted, the discussions focused primarily on the continued functions of the rule, rather than its origin. Neither the tautology involved nor the absence of an origin explanation is a reason to dismiss the arguments of contemporary sociologists. However, where they are seriously deficient is in their almost inexplicable failure to consider the data being generated by colleagues on incest itself. The functional arguments had no room for handling such antisocial behavior, but this does not excuse avoiding its implications. Among other things, a consideration of incest might have advised these social scientists as to whether or not the family or society would collapse under its disorderly weight. This information on the deed was being generated by applied social scientists at the same time that sociological theorists were commenting on the positive, if not the absolutely essential, character of the prohibition. On one hand there was some hypothesizing about the essential nature of the nonsexual nuclear family as a prerequisite to society, while others were struggling with the question of how society managed to survive in spite of what was going on in the nuclear family. It would have been enlightening, especially to the theorists, if the two specialties had taken cognizance of each other.

In point of fact, there is neither objective reason nor available documentation to support the hypothesis that society, or even the family, would collapse in confusion and disorder if incestuous relationships were permitted. To presume otherwise is to confuse rules with behavior, to fail to appreciate that social arrangements as we know them may be only alternatives, and to ignore the facts in favor of hypothetical moralistic abstractions. Put more simply, some sociologists often wrote about the Western family as if they had no personal experience with one. Even if this were the case, the practical knowledge of psychologists and social workers should have persuaded them that behavior in the family often failed to correspond to functional prerequisites. In retrospect, the basic defeat of functional explanations of mid-century sociology was neither their tautological nature nor their concern for the persistence rather than the origin of the prohibition, but rather their failure to consider incest itself and assigning it to the category of deviance and thus not in their province. The denial of interest was not only a theoretical inclination, but also a partial response to the potential disorder incest implied for their vision of the Western family.

This is not to imply that incest, if defined as actual sexual intercourse between primary kin, is rampant in our society. In comparison to other sexual contacts it is the experience of a distinct minority. Less prevalent still are incestuous relationships which result in reproduction and thus generate a situation for the presumed confusion often alluded to. Without discounting the potentially devastating individual trauma involved, no amount of exposé literature should distort the fact that incest is a rare phenomenon. This very rarity evokes the subjective moral response and also provides the objective opportunity to reflect on statements about the presumed social and familial effects of incest violations.

Much of the early literature on incest (see Riemer 1940) was equally subjective in tone by drawing attention to the mentally or physically defective nature of those involved, the negative effects such an experience was likely to have on producing further sexual deviance, and the problems this poses for society. However, this view of incest as inherently pathological eventually gave way to a more reasoned consideration as the evidence on the deed accumulated in a systematic fashion. As an example, one textbook author blandly reports that an investigator "who must remain nameless" uncovered twenty brother-sister marriages in one state. These couples were living apparently undistinguishable middle-class suburban lives, including having children. One of the couples were the children of a previous arrangement of this sort (Hockett 1973:172).[3]

More recently and in a similar vein, a therapist reported on two peculiar but enlightening cases of incest. The first was characterized by the therapist as a case of "stable disequilibrium" (Renshaw 1982: 63) involving a twenty-eight-year-old married woman who regularly visited her widowed father in order to clean his house, cook a meal, and have sex with him. She took no apparent enjoyment in any of these activities, but voluntarily engaged in them, in honoring her mother's deathbed wish to "take care of Dad." The woman kept this sexual element of the relationship a secret from her husband, but otherwise was neither overtly distressed nor guilty about the arrangement. She described her father as a "good and kind man." Nonetheless, she was relieved that his advancing years had dampened his sexual enthusiasm.

The second reported instance involved a nineteen-year-old female college student who, while preparing an essay for an abnormal psychology course, read in her textbook that incest was a "heinous crime." As an immediate consequence of learning that the deed was both pathological and evil, she had a sudden anxiety attack and was taken from the library to the campus infirmary. There it was learned that in apparent innocence she had been having sexual relations with her father and three brothers for the past six years. The initiation of these relationships began with the death of the family's mother, at which point the young girl took over her domestic responsibilities. She stated that she assumed that sex with the father, and then the brothers, was expected of her because "men required it." According to her female therapist, the client was well adjusted and guilt-free until she read about the "horror" of incest (Renshaw 1982:107).

Obviously it could be reasonably argued, though the therapist did not take this line of thought, that the girl was repressing her knowledge of the moral implications of the deed, as well as the guilt and even the trauma, until confronting the concrete authority of a college textbook. However, this personal psychological aspect is not a relevant consideration here; we are more concerned with the sociological implications of familial sexuality. This case suggests that in some situations incest need not produce the social consequences implied by more abstract considerations of the issue. Granted that the absence of the mother also involves special circumstances not envisioned by the familial model. However, other sociological reports indicate that even her presence does not necessarily produce rivalrous destructive results for incestuous families. Although an argument of this sort enters into and adds to what are now troubled waters, it has been suggested by some that father-daughter incest is sometimes acted out with the conscious or unconscious knowledge and collusion of the mother. However, this concern is again not particularly relevant to a sociological consideration of the consequences of incest for the family, in contrast to the motivations of those involved.[4]

From this perspective it has been argued that incest could be viewed as a well-orchestrated "transactional pattern" which entails a shift in traditional family roles in order for the group to continue together (Lustig et al. 1966:33). Specifically, this involves the daughter taking over the functions of the mother, including becoming the sexual partner of the father, which coincides with the withdrawal of the mother as the female authority figure in the household. If these role reversals were not to take place, the families in question would disintegrate. As one commentator puts it, this "reprogramming" is a solution to a "dysfunctioning" family unit (Henderson 1972:311). Another points out that incestuous families are united by very strong bonds so that they may resist intervention by outside agencies seeking to rectify what is perceived of as a pathological situation (Muldoon n.d.).

The rare detailed firsthand study of an extended incestuous family "somewhere in South America" by the anthropologist Peter Wilson (1963) confirms many of these observations. He reports that, as the result of previous moral turpitude on the part of the "Brown" family, which included prostitution by five daughters and liquor-supplying by four sons to visiting sailors, all with the approval of the father, the group was shunned by the community. The fact that three of the daughters contracted venereal disease did not help matters. In addition to the social ostracism of the family from community occasions, the members were, not surprisingly, also cut off from potential external sexual partners in the area. This resulted in incestuous relations among fifteen to forty family members over a thirty-year period. Under such circumstances, the outcome was somewhat disorienting to an outsider accustomed to more familiar arrangements. There is "Jack," for example, who had a daughter by his mother and a daughter by his daughter, which would make Jack father, brother, and mate to his first daughter and grandfather, father, and brother to his second daughter. Now, Jack may have been many other things, but he was not a sociologist, so there is no indication this state of affairs confused him, much less occurred to him in his daily rounds.

Emerging from this sort of bizarre behavior was a conglomeration of relatives united by multiple ties, rather than a standard nuclear family. In the context of communal living arrangements, the children defined all resident adults as social parents and vice versa. In point of fact, the idea of group marriage arrangements so dear to Victorian evolutionists meant that any other relationship except to one's mother was always a matter of speculation. Consequently, it may be unfair in some regards to critique existing notions about the necessary functions of the nuclear family and the incest prohibition with reference to this peculiar case. However, some legitimate points may still be suggested.

First, this concrete example indicates that, contrary to sociological opinion, an absence of cross-generational or sibling sexuality is not necessary for a social unit such as the family to carry out its tasks of socialization. The Brown "family" was crisscrossed with such arrangements and managed this task successfully, albeit in a different fashion. Second, this case suggests that the presumed confusion of roles and statuses, resulting in the collapse of the family, is an untenable proposition, since the Brown unit remained viable over time. Third, the data indicate that the social forms we are accustomed to are just that, rather than the only possibility. The ideal nuclear family and its moral components are successful and prevalent, but not the only social forms. Finally, in a positive tone, since the female members who had engaged in sexual relations with close kin were also able to establish other liaisons with outsiders, this confirms the hypothetical suggestion that familial incest and exogamy are not the same thing.

In response to the potential objection that all of this could not be contained by a nuclear family, reference is made to the previous studies of incestuous families which adjusted to this behavior, rather than disintegrating under a strain. In light of this fact, Bagley (1969) has suggested the recognition of what he defines as "functional incest" as a prevalent form of intrafamilial sex. Bagley's overview, based on a consideration of 425 published incest cases from America and Europe, resulted in the definition of 93 "nonpathological" instances in the sense that incest was a response, allowing the families involved to continue to function as a unit. This category involves what he refers to as intellectually and psychologically normal individuals, most often father and daughter but occasionally brother and sister, contemplating, initiating, and maintaining incestuous relationships deemed a necessity for family survival (Bagley 1969: 514). The features of such families include a strong father figure, relative social and geographical isolation, low economic status, and a dependent mother, unable or unwilling to fulfill her expected female roles. This constellation of factors has led in reported cases to sexual relations between the father and daughter, and a corresponding redefinition of roles, with the tacit approval of all involved. According to Bagley, such families continue to operate over time with minimal social and psychological damage to the participants (1969: 509). Entertaining the possibility that there may be little or no negative psychological effects on the females is, needless to say, a debatable and explosive issue.[5] However, this matter is of no significance in determining whether or not the family remains together and continues to function as a social unit. This continuity may be the case despite a variety of regrettable psychological and physical abuses visited upon family members, which are now recognized as an all too apparent feature of domestic life in industrialized countries.

Leaving this sensitive matter aside and returning to the concern for the incest prohibition, some issues can be more clearly recognized. All the studies cited on incest itself take serious contention with all the statements about the presumed functions of the incest prohibition. One by one, the hypotheses are mitigated or dismissed. The facts simply do not offer support for the hypotheses about what is supposed to happen when incest occurs. Social variations emerge, rather than a single predicted inevitable consequence, that is, the disorganization and collapse of the family. The misguided nature of the functional enterprise has a number of explanations, including the commonly noted fact that this approach to a problem inevitably uncovers some positive results of any social arrangement. This same conclusion is maintained by those interested in the prohibition as well as those concerned with the deed. More important, the outcome, for the theorists at least, was dictated by an inexplicable failure to consider incest as a common enough factor of social life. In this regard, twentieth-century social scientists failed to distinguish themselves from their nineteenth-century predecessors. Both banished incest from the realm of intellectual consideration. For the Victorian anthropologists, incest was a regrettable stage in the childhood of man; for Freudians, incest was an object of fantasy; for contemporary sociologists, incest barely glimmered in their thought as some sort of untenable disorganized state. Even Kinsey, who had the courage to initiate a study of human sexual experience, was nevertheless led to conclude that the deed occurred more frequently in the minds of "clinicians and social workers" than in actual performance (Kinsey, Pomery, and Martin 1948:358).

In addition, commentators from all eras, whether advancing inconsequential asides or full-blown models on the subject of the emergence and function of the prohibition against incest, assumed with no apparent pause or qualm that the human intellect recognized the value of the rule against familial sex and marriage outside of its confines. Until recently, little thought was given to the possibility that humans may be responding to biological laws in conjunction with cultural artifacts to account for the prohibition on incest. To do so requires entertaining the notion that what is considered to be the first moral or cultural custom has amoral roots. Undertaking this approach to the problem is not without its drawbacks. For one, it continues to ignore the fact of incest and offers even less room to accommodate its existence in human affairs. On the other hand, it is difficult, especially in light of the dismal record of other schools of thought, to account for the relative disfavor of biological inquiries into the matter. As one anthropologist frames the issue, the past and present disconcertion with the idea of the influence of natural selection on the evolution of the incest prohibition is "amazing" and a question for a future psychohistorian to take up (Ember 1983:67).

Ours is a society with a long history of accommodating the accomplishments of scientific inquiries and conclusions to its cosmology. Today, even social scientists, who might have some difficulties lecturing on the subject, take grave umbrage and exhibit immediate reaction to any organized attempt to diminish the significance of biological evolution and natural selection as factors in the emergence of our species. To deny the implications of these same processes on human social and cultural affairs in general, and the incest prohibition specifically, indicates that such notions must run counter to some deeply held beliefs about human nature. The contribution of the biological sciences to a comprehension of human behavior must begin at some crucial point to be taken seriously. This expansion usually implies impinging on academic boundaries and a subsequent rush to the intellectual ramparts by those who have traditionally claimed the area as their own. Speculation on the incest prohibition now appears to be the sensitive point of attack and defense.

The battle lines between biology and social science are once again arrayed in a now centuries-old conflict. The increasingly sophisticated verbal missiles are in the air. To take shelter would be to miss the excitement. Less apparent than the academic blood-letting is the possibility that if those with a biological orientation to the problem are correct, this will inevitably lead to a subsequent conclusion about the origin of incest itself. Taken together, these resolutions will require a revision of customary thinking about nature, culture, and the human condition. As Marcel Mauss put it, in what he characterized as a "polite" paraphrase of Goethe: "Now the unknown is found at the frontiers of the sciences, where the professors are at each other's throats . . ." (Mauss 1979:97).

CHAPTER 5

The Nature
of the Solution (I)

It is very rare that the passion of love is developed within
the circle of individuals to whom marriage ought to be
forbidden. There needs to give birth to that sentiment a
certain degree of surprise, a certain effect of novelty.

BENTHAM, 1950

THIS EMINENT MORAL philosopher may have confused lust with love,
but he was perceptive enough to consider the possibility that morality and custom may come after inclination. As such, he exemplifies
a quite different approach to the comprehension of human behavior, which has had its effect on the interpretation of the origin and
function of the incest prohibition. For Bentham, the rule against
sex within the family would emerge from or at least coincide with
the sentiments preceding it. Thus the prohibition's regulatory function would merely be in support of this emotional disinclination.
From this perspective, culture as a dynamic intellectual force would
have had no direct impact on the emergence of the rule which was,
and often still is, perceived of as what makes our species *Homo
sapiens.* This appellation implies that we think and then act, while
Bentham's proposition suggests much the opposite.

Those who may have some difficulty in imagining or appreciating
an explanation for the incest prohibition which excludes a cultural
recognition of its advantages as a factor in its emergence or persistence seriously underestimate the inventive capacity of the human
intellect when it comes to interpreting human behavior. Across the
spectrum of theories on this topic, there is even one which goes be-

yond this utilitarian approach by not only excluding a recognition of the rule's cultural benefits, but even finding human physical inclinations and emotional sentiments as irrelevant factors in accounting for its emergence and pervasiveness. This argument required some originality and ingenuity of thought, making it worth considering before setting at Bentham's more complex intellectual legacy.

The possibility that primitive humanity could not have inbred as a norm, due to demographic characteristics compelling the opposite, was first suggested in a brief and modest communication to the *American Anthropologist* by Wallis in 1950. By projecting the existing sex ratio of births into prehistoric times, he argued that in only fifty percent of the cases would a child encounter a mate of the opposite sex and appropriate age in the family for mating purposes. On the other hand, with "the assumption of a sufficient number of families in the group" (he does not specify a figure), there would be the possibility of sufficient partners for complete outbreeding (Wallis 1950:277–278). As a consequence of these figures, he predicted backwards in time that finding a mate outside of the nuclear family would have been the majority pattern for the species. Although Wallis was not convinced that this custom would have social advantages recognized by those involved, he argued that if indeed it did, then this observation would have come after rather than before outbreeding. He concluded his excursion into the dim past with an equally dim estimation of the sociological ken of our ancestors with the statement that this was all a "guess" and, "To paraphrase Lord Timothy Dexter, it seems to be a time for guessing . . ." (1950:279). Wallis's argument disappeared with hardly a ripple and his name, even among those interested in this very subject, became as obscure as the aristocratic authority he invoked in his cause.[1]

This was not the case, however, for his idea, for it resurfaced, albeit with some embellishments, only nine years later in the same journal as an extended article by another advocate of this demographic proposition (Slater 1959).[2] In this instance, the author considered and rejected the familiar arguments of some predecessors apparently better known than those of Wallis, and then suggested a "material cause" for the absence of intrafamilial sex and a resulting pattern of outbreeding. This material cause was extrapolated from presumed early prehistoric data on birth, fertility, and maturation rates in conjunction with those on life expectancy and birth order. The consequence of these factors, Slater argued, would mean that, for the majority, it would be impossible for the members to find a mate within their nuclear family. By the time the children reached sexual maturity, their parents would be either beyond reproductive capacity or dead, as a consequence of the rudimentary conditions of existence. According to her hypothetical figures, there would be a greater possibility of brother-sister mating, but this would only be practical for a minority, due to the statistical rarity of a sibling of the opposite sex of the requisite age. Taken together, this would mean that at maturity the young would be propelled outside of the nuclear family in the search for a sexual partner. Thus the author suggests that intrafamilial mating was originally nonexistent, rather than prohibited, and the rule supporting this pattern would follow from the behavior, rather than the opposite way around.

This Wallis-Slater scenario presents a quite different and less spectacular image of the prehistoric past in comparison, for example, to Freud's primal horde. In this instance, dreary statistics, rather than sexual urges, have to be considered. In addition to the supposition of decreased patricide rates, the argument has other positive features. For one, it allows for this profound pattern of outbreeding to emerge without any sociological or biological sophistication displayed on the part of primitive humanity. This line of thought is a contentious one for those favoring alternate hypotheses based upon a recognition of the prohibition's debatable benefits. Nonetheless, the demographic approach is an attractively elegant proposition to entertain, since it resolves by dismissal many of the problems inherent in other arguments on the same score. Yet the demographic position is not without serious defects, relating primarily to the validity of the statistical data, which are purely conjectural.

For whatever reason, the Slater restatement of the Wallis hypothesis garnered some attention and response.[3] One critique immediately noted that sexual behavior obviously precedes the ability to reproduce. Thus sexual activity or incest could have been a feature of the early human family, even if later rendered impossible by the death of the parents (Moore 1960). Although unwilling to grace early human behavior of this sort with the term "marriage," this

telling rebuttal indicates Slater also confused sex with "mating."
Clearly sex and mating could have taken place, even under the conditions she imagines. Her demographic projections have also been
called into account. Harris, a contemporary proponent of the alliance theory, argues that, from what we know about hunter-and-
gatherer economies today, presumed by Slater's scenario, it is not
safe to conclude that there was a subsequent increase in life expectancy and a decrease in infant mortality with the onset of primitive agriculture, which followed. The hunting-gathering economic
system, Slater presupposes, conferred no distinct mortality disadvantages in comparison to rudimentary agricultural techniques. It
has been proposed that in its incipient stage this succeeding economic form could arguably have resulted in increasing mortality
and decreasing life expectancy for those involved, due to the vicissi-
tudes of simple farming methods (Harris 1977:15). As a consequence, Slater's vision of the inability to find a long-term mate in
the nuclear family could have conceivably carried over even into our
own century in certain parts of the economically underdeveloped
world. The obvious fact that such societies already have behavioral
or cultural rules against familial sex suggests quite clearly that their
absence is unrelated to her hypothetical demographic characteristics.

Furthermore, Slater's unrefined average life expectancy figures fail
to take into consideration the sizeable proportion of the population
which would still live to advanced years. For males, at least, this
would still entail the possibility of continued fertility and reproduction with female offspring (Washburn and Lancaster 1968). Finally,
a reanalysis of the presumed figures by two demographers subsequently concluded, on the basis of more refined statistical techniques, that only three percent of the population would not have a
potential mate within the nuclear family some time during their
reproductive years (Busch and Gundlach 1977). In sum, the demographic argument for the potential impossibility of incest among
primal humanity is not supported by the demographics. Thus the
tempting elegance of this argument is far outweighed by encum-
brances too debilitating to ignore.

This has not deterred others from attempting alternate approaches
to a solution similarly excluding morality and a recognition of the
advantages of outbreeding in accounting for the incest proscription.

As a new paradigm for the study of social life, relying on Darwinian and genetical currents, it is inevitable that sociobiology offer an account for the continuing enigma which it presumes eluded social science. "Avoided" is a key word here, for a basic proposition to emerge was the conclusion that incest was and is avoided, rather than prohibited, since this psychological reaction confers selective biological advantages to any species, including our own. Not surprisingly, this school of thought has a firmer grasp of the implications of genetics and biology in constructing an argument. However, the complexities of cultural systems often elude its grasp. Just as social scientists often espouse folk science in their discussions of incest prohibitions, sociobiologists incorporate folk social science in their own pronouncements.

This all too common occurrence is typified by Edmund O. Wilson, the patriarch of the proclaimed new science of behavior, when he wrote in all innocence:

> Incest taboos are among the universals of human behavior. The avoidance of sexual intercourse between brothers and sisters, and between parents and their offspring is everywhere achieved by cultural sanctions. Where incest does occur at low frequency in less closed societies, it is ordinarily a source of shame (1978:36).

This statement contains three essential points, and all are in error. First, however defined, incest taboos are not human universals. Second, they are not achieved everywhere by cultural sanctions. Third, incest is not ordinarily a source of shame. The cultural complexities on these matters, alluded to earlier in this discussion, are transformed by Wilson into untenable uniformities. This is not a propitious state of affairs for a new beginning. My intent, however, is not sociobiology baiting; many textbooks in the social sciences have also espoused these same misguided assumptions. What is more relevant, this new discipline offers a restatement of the problem by returning to an interest in the origins of the incest prohibition, rather than studying the contemporary state of affairs. In this regard it is possible to be more sympathetic to sociobiology's vision. Whether or not recent converts to this new field have provided a satisfactory solution to the mystery is still moot. A final judgment is best reserved until after tracing the intellectual roots of this non-cultural view of the origin of the rule against incest.

Edward Westermarck, in the late nineteenth century, was the first to explore systematically the possibility of a human aversion to incest as the initial source of the prohibition. As a vastly underrated figure on this particular topic, as well as in terms of his varied contributions to anthropology in general, Westermarck deserves a revival. Although initially attracted to evolutionary schemes and customary survivals as clues to the past, Westermarck quickly abandoned these notions as unsubstantiated by evidence. Instead, he turned to the evolutionary biological ideas of Darwin and to his own insistence on an understanding of customs in their general context. The first influence led him to compose the three-volume *The History of Human Marriage*, published in 1894. The second assumption later compelled him to initiate extensive fieldwork in Morocco. In the process, he lived among the people for two uninterrupted years, learned both Arabic and Berber, "went native" as much as possible in clothes and habitat, and in his publications adopted a then uncommon functional interpretation of native customs (Westermarck 1914, 1916, and 1926). These accomplishments have brought him relatively little attention today, while his theory on the origin of incest avoidance, though well noted then, is often now casually dismissed or entirely ignored.[4]

As a person and scholar, Westermarck is far too interesting to remain in obscurity. For example, his *The History of Human Marriage*, which set forth his ideas on the avoidance of incest, went through five emended editions. In addition, he published an abbreviated version for popular consumption and, finally, a volume on the future of marriage (Westermarck 1926 and 1936). If stacked one on top of another, his books on this subject would extend from floor to ceiling. Yet he himself never married. Indeed, he seemed to have had a positive aversion to the institution. Westermarck reports in his autobiography (1929) that on two occasions during his travels, recently met unattached females began to show signs that he might be an acceptable mate. According to him, one brief acquaintance even proposed marriage, which set this lifelong student of the arrangement aback, since it was his understanding of history and custom that men were supposed to take the initiative in these matters. Dispensing with theoretical issues, he solved the problem in concrete fashion by showing the lady in question a picture of his sister and her children, which he always carried with him on his travels. He then proceeded to explain that the woman in the photograph was his wife and the children were his own. For this breach of the moral categorical imperative, Westermarck asked for Kant's understanding rather than the Almighty's, indicating that to him ethics were a practical social matter. Philosophy aside, this ruse was rather ironic behavior for a scholar who spent his entire life defending the proposition that there was a natural sexual aversion between brothers and sisters.

His arguments on this subject were more straightforward than his behavior. He prepared them initially for his doctoral dissertation in Swedish, and then expanded them greatly for publication in English in the previously mentioned three-volume study. Westermarck managed this erudition and industry while he was still in his twenties. As a result, during his early years in England, colleagues who had invited him to their university for lectures, and who had never met him before, often intially assumed that the grand master had sent his son instead. Time did catch up with him, though, for he was still defending his major thesis over forty years later (Westermarck 1936).[5] His ideas had clearly created a stir, and in lighter moments he was willing to accept mischievously the interpretation of his argument as the proposition that "monkeys had invented marriage." His actual arguments, often misinterpreted, were somewhat more scholarly and complex.

As indicated by his interpretation of his own social behavior, Westermarck had little sympathy for religious doctrines. For his inquisitive and analytical mind, they were deemed too irrational and the mark of an undisciplined intellect which, in contrast, had to seek practical solutions to moral problems. In that context Westermarck was overwhelmingly impressed by evolutionary biology, and in particular Darwin's ". . . explanation of the appearance of purpose in organic life without calling in the aid of the hypothesis of a providence that has created the world according to a certain plan drawn up after a human pattern" (Westermarck 1929:79). For Westermarck, this implied that human customs should be approached from the same perspective. This required seeking some rational explanation for what society deems as moral behavior. The interrelatedness of the universality of the nuclear family, the prohibition of sex within it, and the rule of exogamy enjoining marriage outside of it became an excellent test case for his rational interpretation of the origin of human institutions. For Westermarck there must be some practical explanations for these arrangements, and he sought those in his study of biology, emotions, animal behavior, and human culture.

In the process, Westermarck dismissed the ideas of the proponents of a previous human stage of sexual promiscuity and group marriage, as well as the existence of behavioral survivals of such states as "baseless conjecture" (1921, Vol. II:79). To his mind, there was no acceptable evidence in the historical or ethnographic record to substantiate such propositions. Whatever customs are encountered among a people should be presumed, according to his functional interpretation, to have contemporary, rather than survival, value. In light of the fact that the family and marriage were universal, Westermarck concluded that these arrangements have always been features of human social organization. He also felt, on the basis of his knowledge of animal societies, that this was a demonstrable contention. Although recognizing the difference of opinion during his time, he adopted Darwin's opinion that close inbreeding was detrimental to a species in contrast to cross-fertilization. He therefore concluded that the aversion to incest had a biologically adaptive advantage. Thus Westermarck was not above chiding Darwin for listening to the likes of McLennan and Morgan about the possibility of a human reversion to a primordial state of promiscuity, rather than following his own original inclination on the subject. For Westermarck, the wellspring of the family as an arrangement for reproducing and rearing offspring which precedes marriage as a social bond could be deduced from human biopsychological inclinations. Relying on the assumption that sexual selection was influenced by aversion as well as by preference, Westermarck was led to conclude that inbreeding was naturally avoided, rather than prohibited for moral or recognizable reasons. This implied that seeking a sexual mate outside the family was a proclivity in some undefined and broad sense of the concept. This vague reference to instinct was to cause Westermarck some trouble in the future, since it was an undemonstrable factor to his opponents. However, before we engage the particulars, Westermarck's exact and more pertinent remarks bear repeating, since as of late his reasoning has come in for revival as well as for renewed opposition. The provoking words were:

> Generally speaking, there is a remarkable absence of erotic feelings between persons living very closely together from childhood. Nay more, in this, as in many other cases, sexual indifference is combined with the positive feeling of aversion when the act is thought of. This I take to be the fundamental cause of the exogamous prohibitions. Persons who have been living closely together since childhood and as a rule near relatives. Hence their aversion to sexual relations with one another displays itself in custom and law as a prohibition of intercourse between near kin (1926:80).

The implications of this statement are many. First, in contrast to other arguments, it directly confronts the issue of sex within the nuclear family and its prohibition as the outgrowth of behavior then converted into custom and morality. Second, the hypothesis diminishes, if not eliminates entirely, the significance of culture as an active factor in the human design. For Westermarck, any explanation for the value of the avoidance pattern would come after the fact. Thus, just as Darwin banished the Almighty from a role in physical evolution, Westermarck dismissed the almighty human intellect from playing a part in social evolution. Finally, an account of the origin of the incest prohibition was an explicit aim of Westermarck's overall program, rather than an aside dictated by the presumption of previous stages of promiscuity and group marriage. As such, his work provided a detailed and systematic treatment of the problem, initiating in response an equally organized opposition which stimulated others, such as Durkheim, Freud, and Malinowski, to seek alternatives and, to their minds, more satisfactory hypotheses. Some of these have already been considered, but their implicit or explicit reactions to Westermarck deserve mention.

These responses, now standard fare, can be reduced to two major points expressing obvious difference with the Westermarck hypothesis. The first, posited by Frazer (1910:77), inquired quite reasonably that if there were no natural inclination to commit the deed, why would the prohibition against incest exist? The Frazerian retort seems to point to such a glaring fallacy of reasoning that it is hard to imagine how it could have gone unconsidered by Westermarck himself. However, it should be equally clear that Westermarck was no simpleton. He was a man of many parts, but obvious stupidity was not among them. This very question of the prohibition of a disinclination, which Frazer refers to, was considered by Westermarck. Indeed, this matter was a basic philosophical concern of his entire career. This intellectual process was explicitly considered in the work on marriage, but also formed the foundation of his subsequent two-volume treatise, *The Origin and Development of the Moral Ideas* (1906–08), which took up the prohibition of a wide variety of potential human activities.

The fact that Westermarck had consciously entertained the question does not imply he provided a satisfactory answer to his contemporary critics, who in the main seemed to be aware of his overall concerns. However, this appreciation of Westermarck's intellectual subtlety appears to have been lost over time, and today evaluators seem to be oblivious to any more than his statement that physical familiarity breeds disinterest, as if it were the sum total of his inexplicably bizarre thinking. As a consequence, present critics hurl back at Westermarck his very own reservations, as if these had gone unconsidered by their originator.[6]

Ironically, in partial response to one of his early critics (Durkheim 1963), who suggested that Westermarck's notion was untenable because it would imply eventual sexual disinterest between spouses, he agreed that theoretically this might be the case if they lived together long enough (Westermarck 1926:86). As mentioned, Westermarck may have had no practical experience with marriage, but he was no fool when it came to an intellectual appreciation of the arrangement.[7]

The second explicit attack on the Westermarck hypothesis came, not surprisingly, from Freud in the context of his own theory of the origin and function of the incest taboo (1950). Freud's version of the direct cause of the proscription is admittedly neither satisfactory nor rarely subscribed to in any literal sense, even by his contemporary followers. His suggestion, though, that an unconscious Oedipal myth characterizes the human psyche is both more admissible and pervasive. Westermarck's aversion hypothesis allowed no room for this emotional phenomenon, which functions as a cornerstone of psychoanalytic theory. As such, Westermarck's ideas drew Freud's intellectual wrath. Referring to Frazer's "excellent" early critique, just noted, which implied a human attraction to incest kept in check by the taboo, rather than an aversion, Freud declared that this sexual compulsion was also supported by the "findings of psycho-analysis." He notes, in addition, that the necessary repression of these incestuous impulses cannot be overestimated as the cause of neuroses in later life. He concluded, therefore, that Westermarck's views are untenable and "must be abandoned" (Freud 1950:122–124).

Westermarck, however, was still alive at this time, and he never swayed from his philosophical commitment to the general premise that aversions lead to customs and moral judgments, nor from the particular one on incestuous avoidance. Subsequent editions of his 1894 book allowed him the opportunity to take on all the reigning masters of social sciences, with what must be deemed varying rates of success. For Westermarck, this reconsideration involved the soundness of counterproposals with reference to the existence and quality of evidence, which he evaluated in comparison to the original and subsequent material he generated for his own position (1929).[8]

Remembering that this was a time when psychoanalysis was still an intellectual novelty, not yet an integral part of our view of human nature, Westermarck responded to Freud by simply remarking that he had yet to be convinced there is any "evidence" of repressed desires to commit incest. This was a "supposition," derived from Western myths and the unconscious of neurotics, rather than an "unearthed fact." Westermarck did not believe these sources of data should allow for a conclusion that similar unconscious themes existed in other societies, past or present. For his own part, Westermarck referred to the lack of incest, which he believed was more apparent from the record, in contrast to a strong unobserved desire to engage in it. In the process he commented on the scattered evidence from human and animal behavior, which supported his contention of sexual disinterest among familiar individuals.

Turning to Durkheim's objection to the argument's implications for a potential dulling of sexual interest, even among the married,

Westermarck observed, in addition to his previously mentioned insight, that he was concerned with the attitudes of those raised together, as opposed to those who married as mature adults. These were entirely different contexts, calling forth varying emotional responses. As with his encounter with Freud and others, Westermarck did not take the easy opportunity to turn the process around and attack his opponents' own dubious explanations for the origin of the taboo. Instead, he politely ignored Durkheim's argument that the incest taboo could be understood in terms of primitive humanity's presumed fear of blood which contained the totemic spirit.

More concerned with the strength and validity of his own premises, rather than the propositions of others, Westermarck responded in similar fashion to Frazer, especially since this critique, which struck at the heart of the issue about the basis of morality, had been adopted by others. For Westermarck, Frazer's contrary opinion that the law forbids what men wish to do was a curious misconception of the origin of legal prohibitions. On the particular score of prohibited sexuality, he believed Frazer's line of reasoning would also lead to the conclusion that humans were naturally inclined toward sodomy and bestiality, which was prevented by even more stringent regulations. Westermarck admitted that these deeds, as well as incest, also occur, but this is no indication of a general human propensity to engage in them. Westermarck argued that he was primarily concerned with behavioral generalities, rather than rarer perversions. His overall position, in response to many of the attacks, could have been strengthened by reference to the many societies now known not to exhibit a prohibition and correspondingly not beset by incest. However, Westermarck apparently presumed at the time, as did his critics, that a stated prohibition was universal. Nonetheless, Westermarck fared well in the exchange on these two interrelated major points regarding the countervailing assumptions about the unconscious proclivity of the incestuous desire and the rise of the prohibition to combat this propensity.

Frazer also raised an objection to the inability of Westermarck's argument to account for the extension of the prohibition to a wider circle of kin, in which marriage is also forbidden in every society (1910:97). Both Frazer and Westermarck, in response, took this to be a major problem worthy of extensive consideration. As indicated earlier, this is an extraneous issue, since it diverts the topic away from sex to marriage rules, which are often different, so the criticism itself is spurious. This fact also went unnoted by both, so Westermarck was only able to offer a lengthy but feeble response, suggesting that the aversion sentiment was widened to include a wider body of kin. In essence, this was a rather unsatisfactory response to an equally unsatisfactory objection to the basic argument.

Frazer, however, continued his attack in a more sensitive area by quoting Westermarck's bald statement: "Human marriage appears, then, to be an inheritance from some ape-like progenitor" (Frazer 1910:96).[9] Westermarck's strategy of considering a possible coevolutionary link between animal and human social behavior was quite unacceptable to Frazer. Moreover, his opponent's reliance and even overextension of Darwinian biological principles about the positive effects of outbreeding as a function of the aversion showed a serious failure to appreciate what distinguished man from beast. In grave tones, Frazer advised that Westermarck and his like, who fail to take into account human "intelligence, deliberation, and will" in shaping social destiny, are not practicing science "but a bastard imitation of it" (1910:98). This admonishment was a telling departure from his normal method, since Frazer offered no evidence for this proposition. The words were more of a statement of faith and a warning to those who would diminish the significance of human cultural capacity and the direct contribution it made to the promulgation of the incest prohibition. This was consistent, though, for someone such as Frazer, who subscribed to the idea of continued intellectual evolution as a definition of human nature.

For his part, Westermarck ignored such attacks on his failure to award sufficient prominence to human intelligence and culture, and continued to "emphasize the facts," rather than concern himself with their heretical implications. To him, his position allowed for an elegant accounting of three profound phenomena. These were the avoidance of intrafamilial sex and the resulting rise of exogamy, which together precluded the negative consequences of inbreeding. He never swayed from this intellectual path and in the end, reflecting on its notoriety, sanguinely referred to his "marriage" to these ideas as one which brought "many roses" (1929:99).

Westermarck had little reason to be so self-assured for, despite other honors, his ideas on this particular subject failed to catch hold during his lifetime and immediately thereafter. In retrospect, there were many soft areas which protruded from his model. His allusions to instinct and sentiment as the causes of the aversion to incest were never spelled out or capable of demonstration. The successful attack on instinctual arguments as the inspiration for human behavior by social scientists in a subsequent area inevitably cast a cloud over Westermarck's argument. His equally vague references to the supposed "horror" reaction to the incestuous deed and the presumption of universality of the prohibition were also misguided assertions. The same could also be said for his linkage of sexual prohibitions with marriage rules. Finally, his argument had little to offer in the way of an explanation for the fact of incest. In many ways, the deed was even more troublesome, since for Westermarck the absence of such behavior was a consequence of an instinctual aversion. As such, incest fit uncomfortably into, if not denied outright by, his theoretical model. His postulation of "vitiated instincts" (1971:365) to account for instances of incest has little explanatory value. Yet on most of these issues Westermarck was hardly distinguishable from his contemporaries. Therefore his relative neglect can be deduced primarily to the contemporary rejection of his dismal view of human nature. This outlook on humanity became exceedingly more unfashionable with the rise of the social sciences, whose concerns and answers provided more positive contrasting images.

The mere fact of being out of intellectual synchronization, and thus languishing in relative obscurity, as compared to Freud, Frazer, and Durkheim, who were more attuned to their times, does not necessarily imply Westermarck deserves resurrection. Many thinkers have thoroughly earned their neglect, but Westermarck is not to be counted among them. His ideas were at the same time too basic and original, and thus intellectually nettlesome, to earn perpetual rest as long as the incest prohibition remained a live issue. Though somewhat timorously at first, his name began to make a reappearance in academia, especially among anthropologists who, in America at least, continue to pay service to the notion of their discipline as an all-encompassing study of human nature, including its biological components.

Faithful to Westermarck's continued concern for the nature of the evidence, anthropologists began to see in the data new support for the aversion hypothesis. Rather than choosing ethnographic instances from here and there for brief mention to shore up a position, characteristic of Westermarck's procedure as well as his opponents', contemporary students focused on a few cultural examples. As the instances of incest tended to show the weaknesses of functional statements about the prohibition, the absence of the behavior in the form of a lack of inbreeding among biologically unrelated but close associates indicated to some that sexual avoidance was an operational principle. If this was the case, then Westermarck would be vindicated. No one had more to do with rolling back the stone over Westermarck's resting-place than Robin Fox, whose apostolic work appeared in a number of publications.[10] These will be attended to, but two particular informative cultural situations deserve immediate and singular attention before returning to the general problem.

The information bears directly on a contention raised earlier by Frazer that "Neither sentiment nor law forbids the marriage of persons who have been brought up from childhood together, and such marriages are probably not uncommon" (1910:97). Westermarck responded to the charge with scattered references to situations in which community exogamy prevailed, even though marriage rules would have allowed for such unions. As indicated, Frazer had unwittingly switched the topic from sexual activity to marriage regulations, but Westermarck nonetheless took the bait in a subsequent edition (1929). His haphazard tribe-trotting procedure was ultimately unconvincing, since contrary instances were just as easy to come by, even in the vague ethnographic atlas of the times. However, subsequent, more systematic investigations by others into the sexual and marital inclinations of Israeli kibbutz residents and the analysis of a particular traditional Chinese marriage form offered more promising grounds for a test of the Westermarck effect.

The Chinese example involves a consideration of the response of those involved in arranged marriages between virtual strangers, in comparison with the effects of similarly arranged marriages between biologically unrelated couples who were raised in the same household from infancy or early childhood. Although not a controlled experiment, the data have been interpreted by some as offering the possibility of estimating the significance of Westermarck's aversion hypothesis. This procedure involves an interpretation of the emotional and attitudinal reactions of the parties involved in each type of union. These were considered in conjunction with the analysis of the varying statistics on divorce, adultery, and birth rates of each marriage form, which were construed as indications of the couple's sexual satisfaction with the marriage.

The union of the familiar individuals, called *sim-pua* marriage, was achieved by the parents of a boy adopting an infant female of approximately the same age (usually at a year old or younger), with the express intent of marrying the two sometime after puberty. Thus the children were raised together and, as such, psychologically like brother and sister. This context stands in stark contrast to the opposing, more prevalent marriage form, which united a couple who may never have seen each other until the day of the actual nuptials. The qualitative and quantitative evidence on the contrasting arrangements, derived from informants' statements and demographic data, were considered over an extended period in a series of reports by Wolf.[11] According to the author, the results consistently support the Westermarck hypothesis on the presumption of a sexual aversion to each other by those raised from an early age in close physical contact. The agreement with Westermarck was initially advanced in tentative fashion. However, in the final presentation equivocation disappeared with the author's closing statement that the only justifiable conclusion to be derived from the evidence was the existence of some feature of childhood association which eventually precludes or inhibits later sexual desire. This implied that the incest prohibition was not a demand of the familial or social order, nor a response to repressed sexual desires. Instead, it should be interpreted as an expression of psychological and physical disinterest on the part of those raised together (Wolf 1970:515).

The data which led to such a conclusion were the statements of parents about the amount of coercion involved in getting the *sim-pua* participants to agree to the arrangement or to consummate the marriage. One father remarked that he had to chase the couple into the bedroom with a stick and stand guard outside to insure that they did not escape (Wolf 1970:508). However, even this did not necessarily achieve the intended results, since 12 of the 132 *sim-pua* couples apparently never had sexual intercourse after years of marriage.[12] The participants themselves referred to the marriages as "disgusting," "embarrassing," "uninteresting," or "meaningless" (Wolf and Huang 1980:89 90). Some of the intended brides refused to cooperate, which meant they remained in the home as spinsters, even after their previously intended husbands were provided with another spouse by their parents. Others were either evicted or ran away to support themselves by whatever means possible.[13] All such responses were considered outrageous in a society known for the expression of parental authority and filial piety, exemplified by the acceptance of arranged marriages between virtual strangers.

The statistical data construed as further support for a strong undercurrent of sexual aversion included the higher divorce rate for *sim-pua* marriages when compared to the other form. The dissolution of the union often took place after the timely death of the parents who enforced the arrangement. For the more traditional marriages, this was a rare outcome, two or three times less frequent than for the *sim-pua* (Wolf and Huang 1980:185). The breakup was doubly significant for the wife, for she could not return to the home of her unknown or unfamiliar biological parents. Thus, in this delayed response to an unsatisfactory situation, the woman was forced into the difficult position of having to fend for herself in a society which deemed such an outcome as unusual and normally unacceptable. Significant for the aversion argument is the fact that the divorce rate for these marriages of social siblings increases in response to the ages at which they were brought together in the household. If they became acquainted with each other prior to four years of age, the dissolution rate was just over twenty percent. This figure decreases to just under ten percent if their proximity did not occur until eight years of age or after.

The statistics on reproduction are also instructive, since *sim-pua* marriages had a fertility rate twenty-five to thirty percent lower than for arranged unions. In addition, adopted females who for some reason did not marry their intended husband, and eventually married another, had more offspring than those who did complete the arrangement. As a consequence, there is no reason to assume that some hidden variable, such as physical mistreatment or deprivation associated with the adoption and rearing of a female child for marriage, affects the fertility rate. Finally, there is the more difficult matter of adultery to assess, since it is based on informants' statements about others in the community, rather than hard data on the behavior derived from those personally involved. Wolf and Huang (1980:146–148) consider the problems involved, but conclude there is no reason to assume that *sim-pua* participants would be the subject of any more negative gossip than those involved in the more typical marriage form. The figures on the number of *sim-pua* women involved in publicly adulterous affairs were always higher than for their counterparts. Depending on the location, this ranged from almost one-quarter of these females in one, to close to sixty percent in another community, in comparison to a high figure of one-third for women engaged in the major marriage form. Overall, *sim-pua* women had a reported adultery rate over twice that of their colleagues who were married to previously unknown males (Wolf and Huang 1980:159). The authors take this behavior to be an indication of a relative lack of sexual satisfaction with a spouse and, in conjunction with the information on divorce and fertility, they conclude that the implications of *sim-pua* marriage lead to a confirmation of the Westermarck hypothesis on sexual avoidance.

As noted, the information on this particular cultural setting was advanced in publications over a twelve-year period. The principal author's interpretation of the data and conclusions have drawn some sharp critical response.[14] The main objection to Wolf's conclusion has come in the form of suggestions about his failure to note some other variable embedded in the *sim-pua* arrangement which could affect the quality and outcome of the union. Specifically, these have included the possible mistreatment of the female in her adoptive household, or the wife's resentment toward the members of it. In considering these objections over the years and reevaluating his data, Wolf was able to ascertain that these were not existing factors. He argues, in contrast, that the unfamiliar bride who enters her husband's household after marriage is far more likely to be the object of negative treatment than the girl raised in it, who is already an accepted member.

On a more quantifiable issue regarding the recognized low status of this form of marriage, in contrast to the other type, Wolf was able to measure the effects of this factor by comparing it to an arrangement of even lower social value. These were uxorilocal marriages, involving the atypical procedure of the husband entering the bride's household at marriage. These arrangements were also considered beneath the ideal. However, Wolf notes in response that these marriages were, in most respects, equal in terms of fertility, divorce, and adultery rates to the more appreciated, opposite living arrangement. Moreover, they were more successful on these counts than *sim-pua* marriages, suggesting their low status could not account for the negative results generated.

Objections to this interpretation by those with less familiarity with the cultural and statistical data are neither unexpected nor unreasonable, in light of the potential to overlook other factors. A single supporting example also presents any argument with problems. However, for those inclined to entertain the aversion syndrome there has been additional confirmation from other ethnographic settings which do not entail the objections alluded to by the critics of the Chinese example. McCabe reports (1983) that the common Middle Eastern pattern of male marriage to the father's brother's daughter initially appears to support the idea that humans are inclined toward sex with close kin, but the outcome actually confirms the opposite position. Although such marriages are preferred by the society in the form of the parents, these unions are relatively unsuccessful on two dimensions previously raised. These marriage partners, who were reared in close proximity in the same community during childhood and who shared many of the social experiences of brother and sister, eventually produce negative results with marriage at a later date. Investigating this patrilateral parallel marriage system in a single Arab Lebanese community, McCabe reports that, first, they were four times as likely to end in divorce than other types of unions between more novel partners (13.04 to 3.2 percent). Second, these unions of familiar kin produced twenty-three percent fewer children than other marriage forms. Furthermore, in order to insure that cousin marriage per se was not the significant variable, in contrast to the presumed one of childhood association, these unions were compared to the other three forms of cousin marriage, such as with father's sister's daughter, and so forth. The latter types, which lacked the significant levels of childhood interaction, had more positive divorce and fertility results, comparable to the marriage of non-kin.[15]

A third, more extensively studied and debated ethnographic context provides further relevant information. The pioneering research on the Israeli kibbutz, which involves the communal socialization of children, drew attention to the high degree of physical and emotional contact between the sexes (Spiro 1958). Boys and girls bathed, slept, and played together, and common enough sexual experimentation was never interrupted or chastized by the adult supervisors. Later during childhood, many of the boys and girls would form couples, which were constantly together. With time and the experience of puberty, the sexes drew apart, however, with the girls displaying physical modesty and the boys showing disinterest in their domestic mates. The initial ethnographer of these collectives drew no implications from this behavior as support for the aversion hypothesis, which went unconsidered. Subsequently he resisted such an interpretation as a potential rationale for the behavior (Spiro 1982:144–159).[16] However, other commentators have been less resistant to this line of reasoning.

An Israeli sociologist explicitly raised the avoidance argument in a subsequent investigation of sexual and marriage patterns among kibbutz mates of the same age (Talman 1964). Noting that data on 492 community members failed to uncover a single marriage among those of approximate age reared together, she concludes that the selection of an out-group marriage partner is an attitudinal or behavioral trend displayed by those involved, rather than one guided by normative rules. She adds that since out-marriage always meant the loss of a community resident to another settlement, the parents would have preferred a union between young co-residents. However, this was never the case, so she presumes this inclination ran counter to parental and community pressure encouraging contrary arrangements. As such, Talman also concludes the pattern exemplified an avoidance syndrome.

Again, not everyone was convinced.[17] Minor objections were raised, but these failed to dampen a growing enthusiasm for recognizing the Westermarck effect on human sexual behavior. Subsequent fieldwork and resulting reports (Shepher 1971 and 1983) on kibbutz mating patterns not only substantiated the previous one, but also sought an underlying causative factor for the phenomenon, which Westermarck had offhandedly laid to human instinct. Confirming the incidence of and relaxed atmosphere toward childhood sexual contacts in the kibbutz, which diminishes at approximately nine or ten years of age, Shepher then analyzed all the available marriage statistics for the entire Israeli kibbutz movement. The data yielded 2769 unions for those raised in collective settlements, but none involved a "true intra-peer group marriage" (Shepher 1971:297).[18] The extent of premarital sexual affairs could not be documented in equally systematic fashion, but Shepher's investigations led him to conclude these were also absent.[19] In addition, the author reports that those who had been affected by the avoidance pattern were not only aware of the process but regretted it, in part because of the effect it had on community solidarity. Their parents found the emotional outcome equally regrettable.

To this point, this research merely offers further tentative support for previous conclusions on an aversion syndrome in another ethnographic setting. Although controversial enough, Shepher breaches a more contentious area by suggesting that this human behavior is the result of "negative imprinting," which he characterizes as the most primitive learning process known, and well documented for animals (Shepher 1971:293). At this stage, the notions of contemporary sociobiology, with its new vocabulary to replace worn-out notions of instinct and sentiment, often evoke a sometimes emotional and acrimonious response. Linking animals to humans has never been an attractive equation in social science, while the study of animal behavior for clues to humanity is looked upon with even more disfavor. Yet this line of reasoning is finding its converts, especially in anthropology. No one exemplifies this approach more than the aforementioned Robin Fox, by the explicit adoption of sociobiological propositions to the study of the incest prohibition.

In his first confrontation with the topic, Fox (1962) aimed at resolving what would appear to be the irreconcilable differences between Freud and Westermarck. Their assumptions—by one that incest is avoided, by the other that it is an attraction—seem to allow little room for compromise. However, Fox manages to effect a marriage of their ideas by arguing in an initial sense, contrary to both parties, that social arrangements, rather than psychological inclinations, lie at the heart of the issue. Whether or not a child will be sexually attracted at puberty to a sibling, or any other person of the same age he or she is raised with, depends upon the quality of their interaction in the early years. Through the consideration of a series of cases from the cross-cultural evidence, including the kibbutz and Trobriand instances, he demonstrates that close childhood association corresponds to a later personal avoidance and an absence of a stated cultural rule against such behavior by the society in question. In contrast, cultural settings which involve a strict segregation of the genders during the early years of cosocialization generate subsequent conscious or unconscious sexual attractions at puberty. Moreover, the society is also characterized by an explicit rule banning the consummation of the desire.

On the one hand, this suggests that Westermarck and Freud were both incorrect by positing universal psychological tendencies without due consideration of cultural factors governing child-rearing practices. On the other, Fox's argument demonstrates that if this factor is integrated with their assumptions, then both can be shown to be partially correct in their basic contentions about incest and the function of the prohibition against it. It is impossible to determine how the masters might have responded to this admirable union of their ideas. As an aside, it would be interesting to consider if the opposed theoretical orientations of Freud and Westermarck did not reflect their own experiences of contrasting cultural systems of nineteenth-century central Europe and Scandinavia.[20]

Contemporary social scientists should not be uncomfortable with Fox's resolution, for the argument gives due credit to both sociological and psychological components of human behavior. At the least, if this thesis were sufficiently noted by others, it would result in the demise of the still oft-encountered statement in support of Freud that there would be no need for a prohibition if humans were not attracted to incest. Among the many advantages of Fox's line of approach is its concern and ability to account for cultural variations. This should also give pause to those who continue to state that the incest taboo is universal. Moreover, Fox's account recognizes the importance of culture, and thus implicitly allows for the existence of both the practice of incest and the prohibition. These are obviously not incompatible phenomena. Finally, the foregoing demonstrates

that it is possible for someone to have an original and still acceptable idea on a topic which has suffered from the continued ad-
vocation of unacceptable axioms as the result of a common and
thoroughly understandable expression of intellectual resignation or
desperation.

Nonetheless, there are some problems with Fox's thesis, which
focuses primarily, as did Westermarck's original, on sibling sexuality, rather than on cross-generational inclinations. Therefore it should
be mentioned that, for Fox, close physical contact between child
and mother in conjunction with the rejection of advances leads to
a learned avoidance of this parent as a sexual object. In contrast,
the relative absence of physical contact between father and child
leads to this as the most prevalent form of incest (1962:149).
Again, this skirts, rather than confronts, the possibility that different explanations, rather than one, may be needed for both potential incestuous relationships, as well as for the prohibitions against
them.

Fox's explanation for the avoidance response, however, has invited some reservations. In the initial publication, avoidance was
laid to early frustration because of the inability to achieve sexual
satisfaction, due to physical immaturity. As such, this experience
with a sibling provided "negative reinforcement," which in later
years leads to a "positive aversion" to each other and attraction to
a potential sexual partner outside of the family (1962:132). However, in a subsequent publication Fox's revised explanation suggests
heresy as the result of a conversion to sociobiology, since he argues
that learning in the form of psychological conditioning is unimpor-
tant in accounting for avoidance. Human cognition as a factor is
jettisoned in favor of recognizing the operation of what he refers to
as "several inbuilt mechanisms" leading to a natural avoidance of
incest. According to this revised version, these crucial elements are
derived essentially from the process of biological evolution (1980:
215). A commitment to this line of thought obviously invites more
concerted attacks from social science, but this need not be evidence
of a failing. However, there is a problem from the perspective of an
interest in accounting for incest. Fox is inevitably led away from
this previous concern. By now suggesting that incest is avoided and
rare because "we are primed not to do it" (1980:216), Fox simulta-

neously avoids an intellectual confrontation with the behavior he had come so close to accounting for. If there is an "innate" aversion to incest; if we are "wired" to avoid it; if it is a "species specific" adaptation; then how can its existence be accounted for in a systematic fashion?

Incest now becomes even difficult to accommodate. The existence of the deed is obscured not only by reference to genetic structures and biological tendencies, but more recently by the sexual antics, or the more surprising lack of some, by our primate cousins, who are essential characters in the sociobiological scenario. These creatures have come to play no small part in recent controversial interpretations of human behavior and explanations for the incest prohibition. As Westermarck originally suggested, this is best viewed as a cultural rule derived from an innate avoidance. Opining over fifty years ago about whether or not incest is an attraction or aversion, the distinguished early Oxford anthropologist R. R. Marett (1932:59) suggested that proposing to arbitrate between such evenly matched opponents would only "spoil a good fight." Too many words and years have gone by to continue to adopt such a sporting proposition. In addition, the situation has become exceedingly more complicated because it now involves an orchestrated confrontation between man and beast in the inquiry on human nature.

CHAPTER 6

The Nature
of the Solution (II)

We understand them no more than they us.[1]
MONTAIGNE, 1603

THE SOCIAL HISTORIAN Keith Thomas (1983:126) mentions that in the seventeenth century a rural English clergyman claimed to have seen crows "planting" a grove of oaks which they then employed twenty five years later for nesting purposes. Examples of such animal perspicacity became the vogue during that age, in contrast to an earlier era which had greeted any implication of equality between human and animal nature with hostility and rejection. However, by this later date there were many who credited other species with rational thought, exceptional intelligence, and a form of language involving gestures and sounds. Those subscribing to this view assumed that humans simply did not understand animal language any more than the typical European was able to comprehend Japanese. There were also those of the time who suggested that only an idiot would entertain such a doctrine. This situation has not changed much in our time.

A society's view of the distinction between man and beast, or more basically between culture and nature, is no small matter; nor is the issue restricted to those groups or times characterized by a more immediate contact with the natural world. For some period in the history of Western thought, an important distinction between humans and animals was the existence of the soul, which also implied free will and reason. Though God's other creatures partook of the divine plan in some lesser manner, the discrepancy between the

two realms was emotionally marked and intellectually guarded
(Thomas 1983:30–35). However, with the continued seculariza-
tion of thought ushering in a scientific age, the existence of the
soul becomes less relevant as a dividing line between the two creatures. The human soul is replaced by the sudden appearance of the
equally mysterious and difficult to grasp concept of culture as the
distinguishing feature of what are now classified as biological species, rather than divine creations.[2] The recognition of this dichotomy of course precedes our time, but the diminishing significance of
the human soul in academic discourse heightened the relevance of
culture as an inspiration of the creature, rather than its creator.

In this process of redefinition, social science, even more than science, replaced theology as a secular system of thought concerned
with elucidating the mark of humanity. This is not to suggest that
the existence of culture is not a factor worthy of consideration.
However, in some future time it is likely that this concept will
no longer be deemed the proper one for subdividing the world of
living things, and will be replaced by another set of oppositions.
However, until the day culture joins the soul in the museum of
Western thought, it has to be contended with, for today the debate
over the significance of this elusive concept is raging. In contrast to
a previous view, which extended the attribute of culture to animals,
at present the primary thrust is in the opposite direction, as many
now attempt to eliminate or diminish this factor in human behavior. Thus, rather than animals being more like humans, we are often
seen as more like animals. The suggestion that we have less soul and
culture has not rested well with the majority in social science. More
often than not, the issue of the prohibition of incest and the nature
of human kinship provides the area of contention.

As noted, information on other species was occasionally alluded
to in references to the origin of the incest prohibition. In some instances, the biological consequences of inbreeding were noted as
either negative or inconsequential, and, interestingly enough, Darwin was often cited by those on different sides of the issue in support of their contrary positions. In rarer moments, the social behavior of animals was alluded to, and the dominant position on the
subject of their sexual activities was that their patterns inverted
human ones. This included indiscriminate mating, which lent sup-

port to the notion of similar incestuous primal hordes among our ancestors in the mists of time. Such a conclusion did obvious damage to Westermarck's cause, so he suggested at the time that the evidence on animal sexual behavior was too unsettled, while evoking some examples of animal sexual indifference to familiar mates in support of his aversion hypothesis (1929:82–84).

The initial systematic study of primates in the London Zoo by Zuckerman (1932 and 1933), in the first half of this century, did little to undermine the position of those who presumed that animal sexual behavior had little in common with the rules guiding human activity of the same sort. As the result of his observations, he was compelled to conclude that for comparative purposes there was admittedly only a "degree" of difference between animals and human social behavior, but the gap separating them was "immense" (1932:18). For Zuckerman, the variable which distinguished the two species was the human capacity for culture, in contrast to the "physiological" basis of animal behavior. As a consequence, he did not hold with the view of the possible existence of a social continuum which linked human to animal behavior. In contrast, there was a sharp break between the two patterns of social organization marked by the existence of human culture (Zuckerman 1932:19 and 1933:20). In the course of his observations, he also noted some "incestuous" behavior between one mother-son pair of primates (1932:271–272), which likely influenced his conclusions.

Subsequent laboratory and field investigations on more distant species by early ethologists such as Lorenz and Tinbergen, though circumspect in tone, began to cast a shadow over the prevailing assumptions about the uniqueness of human behavior. However, even before the floodgates were opened by a vaster quantity of research on closer animal relatives and by even rasher interpretations in popular publications, some social anthropologists were quick to note the implications of this trend for the prevailing view of human nature. The first to attempt to hold the line against the animal invasion was Sahlins (1959, 1960, and 1976), who continued to maintain an interest in stemming this onslaught as it shifted its base from an ethological camp concerned with a limited interpretation of animal behavior to the then still unchristened sociobiology with its grander appetite for deciphering human behavior. Although

Sahlins admitted to primate social organization as a blueprint for similar arrangements among humans, he insisted on the difference between the two, with the recognition of a "new dimension," which was culture. This human element does not express our primate nature; it replaces it, and for Sahlins this means that any claim of specific continuities from anthropoid to even the simplest human societies "must be summarily rejected" (1959:56).

This position would also specifically preclude any contemporary organizational features of humanity as deriving from prehuman incest avoidance. Sahlins writes: "A most significant advance of early cultural society was the strict repression and canalization of sex, through the incest tabu, in favor of expansion of kinship, and thus mutual aid relations" (1959:57). He based this unbending conclusion on the then prevalent view of primate societies as territorially exclusive and semi-closed; that is, they lack a pattern of mate exchange between groups, so that inbreeding among its members was the sexual and reproductive rule (1959:58). Sahlins was relying on the data and suppositions of students of animal behavior, such as Zuckerman, from some time ago, derived from what are now recognized as less than ideal study conditions. Consequently, it would be ungracious to hold him accountable for what are now recognized as inaccurate conclusions about the natural organizational patterns of our nonhuman primate cousins. The sexual behavior of a monkey in the London Zoo probably bears more of a resemblance to that of a sexual deviant Londoner that it does to a normal animal in the wild. The crucial element which went previously unrecognized was that these animals were conducting their lives in an artificial environment. This cultural setting, as it were, permitted them to act like other "cultured" beings, occasionally characterized by inordinate aggression and indiscriminate sexual behavior. Their cultural setting may not only make this possible, but might have actually encouraged such "animal" behavior.

All the more recent primate studies conducted in natural surroundings, which are considered to be more suitable laboratories, conclusively demonstrate that these nonhuman societies are not socially restricted, nor, as a corollary, are they inbreeding. What we would deem as incest is not a feature of animal behavior, since, for whatever reason, these creatures seek biologically unrelated sex-nal partners. In point of fact, it is worth interjecting briefly that incest, which is our primary concern, is more prevalent among humans than among any other primate species. The implications of this fact will be considered, but for now the evidence on nonhuman sexual and reproductive behavior is of more immediate concern. The implications of these research findings will finally allow for some tentative suggestions about the origin of both incest and its prohibition.

Recent years have witnessed an explosion in the field study of animal behavior. Not unexpectedly, much of the commentary centers on our central concerns with the incest prohibition, but less with incest, and then, equally unsurprisingly, the discussion often leaps to some startling conclusions about human nature. No summary could do justice to the massive amounts of information now bearing on so many species, but some specific implications of this intriguing research can be distilled.

An appropriate point of entry into the literature is provided by the work of Japanese ethologists. Despite initially going unnoticed, they were the earliest to take an avowed interest in natural primate behavior, with the systematic observation of indigenous species. Additionally noteworthy are their assumptions about human and animal nature, which are often at variance with familiar Western ones. As an example, Kinji Imanishi, the dean of Japanese ethology, could write in the 1950s: ". . . we much doubt whether it is possible to judge the human race by the limited data obtained from persons in need of psychoanalysis" (1965:116). Failing to give an inch to Western intellectual fashions, he continues that far too much credence has been given in general to Freudian ideas. Thus he notes another "faulty" Freudian legacy concerning the reputed primal horde. Although the Western psyche may have been mysterious to Imanishi, this was not the case for the behavior of his Japanese monkeys (macaques), based upon years of observation spanning their generations.

The idea of a patriarchal horde dominated by a single male who drove out the juvenile ones, or prevented their mating with females, was not substantiated by his pioneering research. Although silent on other relationships, and possibly reflecting a different cultural concern than Freud's, he notes that mother-son mating was never observed (see also Tokuda 1961–62). Expressing some amazement about why this had not been suggested earlier by Western anthropology, he concludes there must have been a precultural stage of human history when inbreeding was avoided as a social practice. Imanishi had apparently not heard of Westermarck, which suggests, at least, that he had not set out in his research to substantiate a previous hypothesis, so this similar conclusion emerged from his own data and reflection.

A decade or so later, this position was being echoed by European and American students of animal behavior. The substantiating data on outbreeding had accumulated to the point where one could write without fear of contestation that the fable of incest among animals is in direct contradiction to the empirical findings (Bischof 1975:55).[3] This unequivocal statement was derived from the evidence of a variety of studies on a host of mammalian and primate societies in the wild, including gorillas, baboons, and chimpanzees.[4] This avoidance of inbreeding is achieved by a number of observed mechanisms. These hold primarily for mother-son and sibling relations, since multiple matings prior to conception often make it impossible for the observers to determine paternity. This suggests, as alluded to earlier, that a father-daughter sexual prohibition for all primates may involve an entirely different explanation from the one which accounts for the other relationships.

For chimpanzees, the absence of inbreeding arises from the abrupt cessation of physical association with familiar males by the females with the onset of sexual maturity. The females then transfer to other troops regularly or permanently for breeding purposes (Pusey 1980). Among rhesus monkeys, the males are usually the ones to leave their natal group at sexual maturity during the mating season. The few males who do remain during this period also avoid sexual relations with their mothers. When it was attempted on rare occasions by juvenile males, the female successfully rebuffed the advances (Sade 1968).[5] In the case of baboons, the males also emigrate from their original troop at sexual maturity. The observer notes that upon entering a new group, the males direct their primary attention to the females, and these in turn have a more positive sexual attraction to them, in comparison to more familiar mates and other males (Packer 1979).[6] Among the red colobus monkeys of West Africa, both males and females attempt to transfer from their natal group at sexual maturity, though the females are far more successful, since they are readily accepted by the new males, despite physical discouragement by resident females. Males who attempt to enter a new unit are violently opposed by both the females and males of the group, but nonetheless they are occasionally successful at transferring (Starin 1981).

Gorilla society in Central Africa is particularly instructive, since it was this creature, in mythical form, which played such a large part in Freud's imaginary primal horde (1950:125). Firsthand observation shows the male to be a rather docile animal who, rather than being obsessed with the drive, displays relatively little interest in sex (Schaller 1964). More pertinent, the daughter of the dominant male will not mate with him, and without objection will become the consort of the second dominant male, unless this is a full brother. If this is the case, for mating purposes she will seek an even less dominant male who is not a sibling. If none is available in her natal unit, then she will leave it, in search of an appropriate sexual partner from another group. For males, it is reported that they will not compete with another for females who are either their mother, daughter, or full sister. If none other is available in his group, then he emigrates at sexual maturity, to lead a solitary existence until and unless he encounters a female who has also left her group for an acceptable mate (Veit 1982). In sum, the sexual behavior of this beast, including the male, is generally peaceful, orderly, and rather prosaic.

For other, more removed mammal species, similar arrangements reduce, if not preclude, inbreeding. The African elephant provides an instructive example, since it inverts expected notions about the significance of patriarchy in the animal world. In this instance, the herd is dominated by females, and in particular by a single matriarch. Before a male offspring of a member approaches sexual maturity and maximum physical strength, it is forcefully expelled from the group by the leader, with the assistance of other females. In contrast, females are allowed to remain for life. The expelled male lingers around its natal group for some time, even years, suffering constant physical rejection and harassment, until it wanders off, leaving the territorial boundaries of the herd to range over an extensive area, in solitude or in the company of other rejected males. Upon reaching sexual and physical maturity, a male will briefly enter a herd for sexual purposes. However, by this time it is likely the bull will have lost contact with his natal group and, as a consequence, mate with an unfamiliar and unrelated female (Douglas-Hamilton 1975).

Examples of these kinds of organizational arrangements, which eliminate or diminish the chances of inbreeding for close or more distantly related species, could be multiplied at will. The results indicate quite clearly that inbreeding is not a social pattern for those animal species we refer to as the lower orders. Therefore, on this issue of sexual behavior, humans cannot presume a major social advance over animals. As a consequence, it is necessary to dismiss the assumption that human sexuality was brought under control by a major cultural advance in the form of the avoidance or, as usually stated, by the prohibition of incest (Sahlins 1960:80). This position is no longer tenable, so that the constantly sought-after difference between human and animal will have to be found elsewhere. Just as what were once referred to as the lower human social orders were eventually invited into the ranks of the civilized on this score, it now appears other species will have to be admitted to the not very select company. Providing an explanation for this pan-special behavior and determining its implications for the human condition is not as clear-cut.

Some students of animal behavior have been quick to see in this prevailing primate sexual pattern the implications for a natural avoidance of inbreeding among humans, as opposed to a cultural origin of the incest prohibition. The general position of those who have offered an opinion on the matter, and there are many, is that our own species evolved from a common mammal or primate ancestor with a genetic propensity to outbreed.[7] In this, commentators note a variety of social advantages, including the elimination of competitive aggression within the family unit, since this destructive behavior is often linked with sex (Kortmulder 1968 and Parker 1976). In terms of biology, the adaptive advantages of outbreeding are referred to for all species, including our own (Bischof 1975 and Demarest 1977). Before these conclusions can be fully appreciated, another evidential element on breeding propensities deserves evaluation, since it reflects on the Westermarck hypothesis, with particular reference to the idea that familiarity breeds sexual disinterest. This factor is implied in many of the studies of primates in natural settings, but it has also been explored under more rigorous experimental conditions for other species.

One such study follows up on the observation that in the natural setting the prairie vole avoids inbreeding. This sexual disinterest can be overcome under artificial conditions of human design, but the reproductive results are interesting. Thirty-one pairs of siblings, brought together in cages at the age of twenty-one days, eventually produced only two litters (9.4 percent reproductive rate). In comparison, eighteen nonrelated pairs, brought together at the same age, produced fourteen litters (76 percent), while twenty-two stranger pairs, brought together at seventy days, which was after sexual maturity, produced twenty-two litters (100 percent). The obvious conclusion from the study is that related familiar pairs will not reproduce at a rate viable for the continuation of the group (McGuire and Getz 1981). Without reference to reproductive rates, other studies of both primates and nonprimates also conclude that novelty is a strong factor of sexual attraction.[8] Moreover, this inclination is not restricted to the male of the species, for it has been noted that some female primates will also take some pains and expose themselves to physical danger from predators in order to mate with an unfamiliar male (Wolfe 1984). This mobility of the females in these primate societies is interesting to note in light of fanciful expressions of human masculine wanderlust in contrast to the assumption that females are more passive and domestic by nature.[9]

Scientific documentation of novelty as a feature of sexual attraction among animals will hardly attract the undivided attention of the scientific community. Extending this argument to a comprehension of human sexual behavior may raise some suspicious response, but otherwise it causes little stir among the public. Suggesting that aversion in a negative sense and novelty in a positive one have some bearing on the origin of incest prohibition through avoidance, however, is another matter entirely. This final step apparently turns a reasonable suggestion into an inflammatory statement, earning every possible objection, if not making it outright dismissible as an unacceptable hypothesis.

Spanning the gap between humans and animals on this issue

without constructing a bridge with cultural underpinnings has been looked upon as a shoddy and dangerous project by mainstream social science. Moving from the behavior of the prairie vole, deer, mouse, and Japanese quail in the laboratory, through the sexual antics of the baboon, gorilla, and chimpanzee in the wild, to arrive at an eventual conclusion about human behavior and morality involves navigating a tortuous path. Some have made this passage in a single bound, and in the process have earned the exasperated disapproval of others. Nonetheless, the legitimate question remains, Does the Westermarck hypothesis have anything of value to offer?

The observation of the sexual and social behavior of animals suggests quite clearly that we are not the only species to be inclined toward outbreeding, with all the biological and social advantages this entails. All the studies of human behavior in cultural settings bearing on this issue, referred to earlier, substantiate the implication of some aversion to familiar individuals as sexual partners. This also has a measurable effect on reproductive roles. Thus, despite the implications, it seems most reasonable to conclude on this single issue, without giving in to more extravagant claims and extensions which often follow, that humans have evolved with a natural propensity to outbreed, expressed by a sexual attraction to unfamiliar mates. Unless the social setting contravenes this tendency we, as with other species, avoid what is culturally defined as incest. Such a conclusion also may explain in part why certain societies have neither a prohibition or incidence of incest. In these instances, the avoidance pattern is not contravened by other factors which would have to give rise to a specific injunction against inbreeding.

In sum, the avoidance hypothesis is a most elegant proposition to entertain, in respect of the data on both human and animal sexual behavior. The contrasting assumption, that ours is the only species to have evolved lacking an outbreeding tendency, and that instead we culturally generate such behavior, is not supported by the evidence. This conclusion is satisfying, but such an argument is also immensely more convoluted. Although the evidence for the aversion hypothesis is circumstantial, it is crucial to recognize that there are no supporting data for the opposite assumption, that incest was prohibited by a cultural invention. Even those who support such a premise are forced to admit to this fact, since it is assumed that incest regulations entered the human cultural record at a point in time now impossible to ascertain or document. To a great extent, this argument must be accepted on faith, normally as the consequence of a critique of the opposite position on avoidance. Finally, as already indicated, many of the statements about the cultural function of the prohibition are not supported by the studies of incestuous families.

Accepting the aversion position leads to a consideration of two unavoidable attending issues. The first involves determining the complex relation of culture to this set of social phenomena, and the second is simply accounting for incest itself. Despite a natural aversion, there is no doubt that culture is also somehow an involved partner and, more important, if incest is avoided, how can its existence be accounted for? These are not trivial matters. The first is usually addressed in cogent fashion by those inclined toward sociobiology before they attack broader questions about human kinship. The second, however, remains as obscure for them as for those who adopt a contrary starting point. Yet those who advocate the avoidance argument would seem to have a greater responsibility to account for incest, as opposed to the majority who suggest humans are inclined toward this behavior. These arguments may be at a loss for evidence on the emergence of the prohibition, but at least they can reasonably account for the deed. Clearly, there remain problems to be resolved, and although they are initially distinct, a resolution of the two are intertwined and require a different vision of incest and culture.

The cultural contribution to the social matrix can be addressed most immediately by recognizing the initial nature of the aversion hypothesis. Its primary emphasis relates to siblings and by extension the mother-son relationship, since these involve, among primates in particular and normally among humans, the most intense physical familiarity. These relationships of constant interaction prior to sexual maturity apparently have the effect of producing disinterest at a later physical stage, when reproduction occurs. The siblings of the opposite sex seek sexual partners elsewhere, and the male will seek a mate different from either his mother or sister. The mother-son bond is a primary one, derived from biological factors involving birth and nurturing over an extended period. The sister-brother relationship is a social one, derived from the mother and intensified by constant interaction among the three.

The aversion hypothesis makes immediate sense in these contexts, especially for primates, but also for humans in most social settings. As noted, the problem emerges with attempting to include the father-daughter equation with the aversion argument. Among most primates, this is not a biological relationship converted into a recognized social one after birth. Consequently, it is not possible for many species, though it is for some, to determine if father-daughter inbreeding takes place. Fatherhood is a presumption, even for human society, and as such it is based on a cultural, rather than biological, relationship to offspring. As a number of anthropologists have suggested, fatherhood, in the sense of the social definition and recognition of the status, represents a dividing line between human and animal society. As such, the appearance of the status and role indicates a more refined transition from nature to culture (Fortes 1983 and P. Wilson 1975, 1980).[10]

This is a reasonable assumption in light of our present knowledge of primate social organization and behavior, so it follows that sexual relations between this pair may be culturally prohibited rather than avoided, depending on the quality of domestic interaction. If this relationship is characterized by early sexual segregation, then later it may indeed generate an attraction held in check only by an explicit prohibition. For some commentators, the absence of these biological and physical components of the father-daughter relationship account for the inclination to violate the prohibition (Fox 1980:216). Indeed, the Parkers' study of incest offenders in this country indicates that these fathers had little physical contact with their infant daughters, as compared to nonincestuous males. Thus it has been concluded: "The data show conclusively that absence from the home or uninvolvement in the early socialization of the child dramatically increases the risk of sexual child abuse" (Parker 1985:1).

The second cultural contribution to this complex is also variable, rather than universal, since only in some instances are social rules generated against sexual behavior between members of the nuclear family. The existence of an explicit prohibition obviously depends upon cognitive and linguistic capacities that are beyond all other species. We are the only creature able to create abstract regulations governing sexual interaction and extend them beyond the nuclear family without reference to innate avoidance or attraction. As indicated, there is great variability on this matter, since some societies have no such verbal injunction while others may. In addition, some may extend these rules beyond the circle of primary kin to include all cousins, some cousins rather than others, or even all members of the lineage or clan where a relationship is merely assumed, rather than traceable.

The issue of particular extensions of the rule governing both sex and marriage is purely cultural. The common criticism that the aversion hypothesis fails to account for the prohibition of marriage to one cousin and encourages marriage with the other is to miss the point.[11] These rules have no direct bearing on the aversion hypothesis. The source of a particular extension is cultural, based upon the human intellectual ability to create social categories of kin and non-kin with little or no reference to biological facts. The prevailing assumption is that other species do not possess this ability. Therefore, on this issue, human variability is expected to be demonstrated, since a lack of cross-cultural uniformity is the essence of culture. The avoidance of incest within the nuclear family and the prohibition of sex or marriage with some individuals and not others outside of it are unrelated factors. The source of aversion to the familiar is an innate proclivity, while the prohibition of others as sexual or marriage partners is social or cultural in origin. The two phenomena should not be confused and, more important, should not be cited as mutually contradictory evidence. To take a particular, familiar example, in Israel there is no prohibition against marrying a member of one's own peer group in a kibbutz community; it is just not done. However, Israeli laws would prevent the marriage of siblings who have never met, in response to the social recognition of a category of kinship.

In point of fact, there is no end to the human capacity to extend marriage prohibitions with little or no regard for biological relatedness. In the Middle Ages, the Church forbade marriages to the fourteenth degree, which would exclude practically all members of the same class over an extensive area. In addition, there were prohibitions against marriage with affines and spiritual kin, such as godparents as well as their offspring. As a consequence, the majority violated these injunctions and, for the nobility at least, this situation allowed for future annulments (Flandrin 1979 and Fleming 1978). Similarly, in Islam the Koran prohibits marriage between a child and wet nurse and the father of the suckled child and the daughter of the "milk-mother" (Khatib-Chahidi 1981).

In essence, a rule against sex or marriage characterizes human society, and such regulations can be expressed in a variety of ways, as the result of the creation of elaborate social categories having little or nothing to do with biological considerations. The human capacity to be accounted for in this instance is more the ability to generate cultural categories, rather than the prohibition of incest. Therefore, it is not surprising to encounter a society that forbids marriage with someone from the same side of the river, a fact which so impressed Lord Raglan (1940). Apparently anything is possible when the human mind contemplates sexual or marriage prohibitions.[12]

Human culture is responsible for rules, in the sense of verbal injunctions against certain sexual behavior. This capacity to conceive of the permissible and prohibited, rather than actual sexual behavior, distinguishes us from other animals. These conclusions may not be majority views in social science, but neither are they novel ones. Even those approaching the particular problem of incest prohibitions from different intellectual perspectives have come to an agreement that, as with other species, human sexual behavior entails some sort of an avoidance component.[13] The opposing intellectual camps also agree that it is scarcely possible to overestimate human cultural capacity in drawing a line between ourselves and other species. In his continuing joust with sociobiology, Sahlins refers to human culture as a "new dimension," which allows our species to overcome biological patterns (1976:58). Not to be outdone in rhetorical emphasis, sociobiologists such as Lumsden and Wilson (1983) metaphorically refer to culture as the "promethean fire." However, with reference to Sahlins at least, it now has to be admitted that the biological pattern we are concerned with here is the inclination by noncultural animals to outbreed, rather than inbreed. Recognizing this new reality has very different implications from the one Sahlins and others of his per-

suasion intended when considering human sexual behavior. Rather
than suppressing, limiting, and channeling the sexual inclinations
of our kind, culture allows for human sexuality to flourish and take
expressive directions inconceivable and thus unavailable to lower-
order primates, which lack our imagination.

Everyone who has taken the time to reflect on this basic issue,
whether staunch sociobiologist or adamant social anthropologist,
agrees that, first, culture is a unique and profound addition to be
considered in interpreting human social behavior. Second, although
it is not confronted or subsumed by their theories, all admit that
human incest takes place. As one commentator suggests, what we
need is a strategy that handles the existence of both prohibitions
and incest (Harris 1971:289). As indicated, these are intertwined
human phenomena, though often artificially divorced. This leads to
an inevitable conclusion: human culture created incest.

This is not a common assertion, nor is this possibility a particularly pleasant one to reflect upon from a subjective perspective. We
clearly prefer to think of culture as making a positive moral contribution to human conduct. Nevertheless, this deduction about the
human origin of incest seems inescapable. However, it is also an
unfamiliar one, so that the assumptions which underlie the conclusion need to be made explicit, even at the risk of some repetition.[14]

The suggestion that culture is responsible for incest does not
imply that culture is not also responsible for creating an explicit
prohibition where it exists. It must be remembered that this rule
is not universal. As indicated, the rule and the deed are interrelated
but not mutually exclusive matters. As Fox (1962) suggested, those
societies which generate a sexual attraction between siblings of the
opposite sex by their child-rearing practices of strict segregation also
produce explicit prohibitions against incestuous behavior.[15] With
differing child-rearing arrangements allowing for physical contact between siblings, there is no need for such a rule. In these instances,
incest is avoided and therefore not a behavioral issue to be contended with. Culture can thus be viewed in this context as a self-
correcting mechanism which counteracts that which it produces.

An appreciation of the relation between the human monopoly on
culture and incest as its by-product requires bearing in mind that
sexual relations between closely related nonhuman primates are

avoided, since, we assume, they do not possess cultural rules. These species lack what we would call incest because they also lack culture. As far as we know, only humans can conceive of certain activities as pure, shameless, and orderly. We can also imagine the opposite characterizations of behavior and, more important, in contrast to other species, we can act out these very notions with deeds interpreted as impure, shameful, and disorderly. The absence of this cognitive ability is not the only factor to be considered. For other primates in natural settings, the sort of sexual behavior in question is either totally absent or empirically rare. Thus, in contrast to past suppositions, this incestuous activity now calls for mention, rather than commonplace sexual avoidance. Behavior which we translate as incest may be the capability of other animals, especially juveniles, but this experimentation ceases with reproductive maturity.

Significantly, full-fledged inbreeding is more apparent among animals under cultural conditions created by humans in the laboratory, zoo, household, or other domesticated arrangements. Consequently, human culture can also produce incest among other creatures through contact and contamination of their natural social arrangements. As an aside, the continued restriction of animal range, even in the wild, by the encroachment of human culture and the creation of animal reserves might have a similar inbreeding effect on these species, resulting in a population decrease noted under laboratory conditions. Culture and, thus, incest have been features of our existence for some time, resulting in a potential greater tolerance for inbreeding among humans in comparison to other species, which follow the dictates of nature.

Finally, underscoring the intimate relationship between human culture and incest is a fact which confronts us on a regular basis; the deed is well documented for our species. In some cases, incest takes the form of the violation of a stringent prohibition, such as in our society. Yet it occurs with regularity, and deserves some interpretation. In other, more telling, instances incest makes its appearance as a responsibility of the political elite to enact prohibited marriages. Thus the deed becomes an explicit injunction. The word "marriage" is used here, since the sexual behavior involved may be more symbolic than concrete. Whatever the case, the practice or suggestion of incest is an artifact of culture, rather than nature.

Exploring these incestuous instances, as opposed to ignoring them, now seems to be a more reasonable enterprise.

Having caught a glimmer of the origin of incest in the reflection of the unique human capacity to generate rules, to reflect upon them, and then to decide individually in some societies to violate them or, in others, to succumb to the collective will to contravene the rule governing the majority, it makes sense to consider the function and, more important, the meaning of incest. Cultural interpretation, rather than dismissal, is called for. This procedure is consistent with the conclusion adopted here, for it is the deed in conjunction with the prohibition which makes us unique. Only humanity can avow that something is immoral and then decide to revel in this condition, out of choice. In essence, the concept of culture is very much like the idea of a soul: it is unique to humans and in expression open to moral judgment. In failing to appreciate this, we may have understood ourselves no more than we understood the other beasts.

CHAPTER 7

The Culture
of Incest

Society expressly forbids only that which society brings
about.   LÉVI-STRAUSS, 1969

THE DISTINGUISHED AUTHOR of this line would obviously not be in
agreement with the position reached in this essay, for, as noted,
Lévi-Strauss views the prohibition of incest, rather than the opposite, as the sign of culture. However, this particular remark on the
origin of social rules finds favor with the argument proposed here.
The conclusion that culture bears the ultimate responsibility for
the appearance of incest may be unsettling to our overly positive
estimation of human nature. However, this suggestion about the
ingenuity of culture does no injustice to the agreed-upon contentions of both sociobiology and social science. The hypothesis suggested here also assumes that we are a species governed by certain
behavioral impulses having adaptive biological and social advantages. Neither camp would find this implication objectionable in the
main.

   This proposition about the origin of incest also recognizes the
ability of culture to overcome these inherent tendencies, shared with
other species, to produce social forms demanding an entirely new
perspective for their interpretation. This position should also be
agreeable to those who approach the problem of human nature
from otherwise different perspectives. Admittedly, the eventual conclusion about the origin of incest, arrived at through the recom-
bination of existing premises, while maintaining a concern for both
the prohibition and deed, is not necessarily self-evident nor ac-

ceptable to the parties to the dispute about how best to interpret human behavior. Both sides seem to place a high premium on human culture. This estimation is not supported by the eventual conclusion of the present argument, which suggests that we are culturally responsible for the act, rather than the prohibition, of incest.

On the other hand, neither perspective has produced a theory which, as others have noted, satisfactorily accounts for all the elements involved, which include the avoidance, prohibition, and commission of incest.[1] This failure of purpose has been pointed out by those who have found themselves disputing almost every other point. The aversion to considering incest in conjunction with an overly positive estimation of human nature has wedded social science and sociobiology, even when their estrangement seemed most severe at a more superficial level. Clearly, a resolution of the problem requires more than a surface compromise between the two orientations. This marriage of ideas is not difficult to effect, but the process requires explicitly recognizing and recasting some implicitly shared assumptions of the two schools of thought. The procedure undertaken here with regard to incest and its prohibition has required neither originality of thought nor new information. The separate elements of the argument were already available in independent form. Any novelty resulted from a redefinition of the problem to admit the act or implication of incest into consideration, and then to reorder the agreed-upon facts to propose not only an explanation but also an understanding of the elusive problem of the prohibition and violation of incest.

The exercise has involved recognizing the failure on the part of mainstream social science, and especially anthropology, since it claims such a broad view of human behavior, to consider the significance of the information on nonhuman societies for an appreciation of the particular problem. This lapse entailed a delayed response to the fact that other primates, as well as more distant species, were clearly outbreeding. This failure was linked with the inability to recognize that human incest might also be avoided in some societies instead of assuming deep-seated attraction to the deed. As psychoanalysis suggests, such a compulsion exists in some societies but it is not apparent in others. This restricted view is particularly mystifying for anthropology, since the conclusion overlooks the potential for cultural variability. The anthropological definition of the problem was, and still is, culture bound, as evinced by the limited consideration of data from other nonhuman as well as human social systems. It should have been apparent that these often fail to agree with the psychological and social experiences of the West.

Maintaining a premise, despite available evidence to the contrary, derives from a profound commitment to basic notions. The assumption that the prohibition of incest was the first cultural act, proclaimed so imaginatively by both Freud and Lévi-Strauss, implied that this very rule was human nature itself. A retreat from such a position does not come easily, since it opens the door to an assault on a variety of secondary propositions also held dear to social science. Abandoning the argument that the prohibition of incest results in the human family as we know it, and sets in motion complex marriage and kinship systems by the search for a mate outside of it, means that the interpretation of these institutions will also be set upon by intellectual interlopers. The emotive significance of the family in both Western folklore and social science, and the practical academic value of kinship systems which have been monopolized as the stock in trade of anthropology, will also have to be defended against by those with a different vision. This battle has already been joined, as sociobiologists now attempt to widen the breach established by confirming outbreeding patterns among other species and interpreting kinship systems and behavior as extensions of other biological principles. Nothing could strike greater horror into the hearts and minds of anthropologists who have distinguished themselves by their portrayal and interpretation of these social arrangements.

However, for those inclined toward sociobiology, the matter is more straightforward, since kinship behavior is also seen as having a biological component. In effect, kinship systems and the activities they generate are based upon, and are reflections of, genetic relatedness. For sociobiologists, individuals who share a similar biological makeup will come to each other's aid in times of crises in order to insure the continuation of their genetic material.[2] Thus morally commendable behavior can be reduced to biological impulses. As one recent exponent of this argument puts it: "If individuals take risks which might effect their physical well-being, they will do so in light of kin relatedness" (Chagnon 1981:39). This is hardly a romantic view of human nature. More and more of what had been viewed and, more important, valued as culture is rendered an amoral genetic function. The issue, however, is not the subjective unattractiveness of such a position, but its intellectual value.

Traditional anthropologists have been quick to defend against this deeper incursion into an arena regarded unique to humanity. Following up on his initial confrontation with sociobiology, Sahlins (1976) has argued—and here he is on firmer ground than in his prior interpretation of primate behavior—that human kinship systems are to a large part cultural arrangements, having little relationship to the biological facts of life. In his view, human cultural ability allows for an extreme reordering of genetic principles. This is achieved through the choice of descent rules emphasizing maternal or paternal kin over the other, or vice versa; the implications of residence patterns which dictate choice of behavior toward one kinsperson and not another of equal genetic relatedness; and the common manipulation of genealogies, so that the social consequences bear little or no resemblance to the biological principles. This leads Sahlins to conclude that, on this issue, culture overcomes biological patterns. Although some have argued (Fox 1979 and Irons 1979) that this human plasticity and flexibility are also features of natural selection, which distinguishes our species from others, this does not substantiate the proposition that kinship behavior can be deduced to be a reflection of genetic principles. On this issue there is too much conflicting evidence from the cultural record to permit such a conclusion. At this point, sociobiology has reached an impasse in accounting for human sexual and kinship behavior.

In this study the question of incest has been defined as a cultural problem. It remains to consider the extent of the practice in the sense of the behavior actually involved, and to examine the meanings assigned to incest by the human imagination. The existence of incest in a variety of forms is a central notion of this argument, but caution dictates a careful evaluation of common claims about its incidence and facile explanations about its purported purpose. This "real anthropological problem," as Schneider (1976) has referred to it, is a rich and complicated one. The failure of some sociobiologists to appreciate that the inquiry involves the exploration of subtle cultural behavior draws attention to the limits of their line of reasoning.

As noted early on, marriage does not necessarily imply sex, and sex in the form of incest does not necessarily result in inbreeding. The deed, or its implication, can be both less and infinitely more than a simple biological act. The enthusiasm that comes with the recognition that both animals and humans tend to outbreed must be tempered by a careful scrutiny of what may be involved when this norm is contravened by our species. When incest is implied, the individuals involved are not only contravening a behavioral tendency; they may also be violating a stated cultural rule. For our species, this cultural component is more significant to contemplate than the biological one. When the act of incest is signified or engaged in, it takes place in the context of a specific cultural setting, so that a symbolic meaning is also at issue. This is not surprising, for the incestuous deed is a trademark of our kind, the only species with a cultural capacity.

This fact has not been appreciated in particular by those who approach the problem of incest from a sociobiological perspective. They interpret this extraordinary cultural behavior as if it were primarily a mundane act of inbreeding in the sense of having reproduction as its main concern. This is a dubious assumption. The opponents, as well as others who may take a more sociological orientation, also fail to appreciate sufficiently an attending methodological problem concerned with the imputation of incest. The suggestion that some groups or individuals engage in this sort of behavior is a common form of cultural slander of some import to those who proclaim it about others.[3] The verbal implication of incest may often be a cultural statement about the inferiority of others. Thus such a suggestion has to be considered carefully before we agree to admit it as evidence of the deed and construct a theoretical argument to account for its existence.[4]

Such imprecations are not only resorted to by one nonliterate people to characterize their neighbors, but it has also been employed in passing by literate societies to justify their cultural superiority. This was a particular, and now recognized, failing of primitive social science, which projected some fanciful sexual behavior onto others in the nineteenth-century world. Having now appreciated that even other species abstain from inbreeding, it would be meanspirited to continue to advocate a salacious characterization of some other human societies. Incest does exist among our kind, but where, when, how, and by whom it is engaged in is a delicate matter, prompting an equally refined mode of consideration. Such a procedure has not always been the case, especially for those who already have a theoretical position to advance and merely lack the evidence in support of their contentions. This sort of prejudgment has often involved entertaining some very suspect ethnographic evidence and reducing all implications of incest to inbreeding and worthy of explanation on biological grounds alone. Such a single-minded approach does an injustice to complex cultural facts.

The problem begins, however, with the utility of the reported ethnography. Typically commentaries, and especially comparative essays, assume that all reported behavior and customs on this topic are equally reliable. For example, in the context of a consideration of incest, one reports: "The Shilluk wink at affairs with a step-mother" (Murdock 1965:285). First, such an arrangement, even if taken to its biological conclusion, would not entail inbreeding, since there is no close genetic relationship between the two. Second, there is no reason to assume, although our cultural system may, that such behavior is deemed incestuous. Third, it is impossible to determine the meaning of the response of others, for it is difficult to imagine that the aggrieved party would react to his wife's and son's behavior with a "wink" of the eye. Finally, there is no reason to conclude that this sexual delict is customary for the people. These preceding points would be little more than expressions of petty academic contentiousness, and reasonably disregarded, if not for the related fact that these African people are also commonly referred to as an example of a society which condones royal sibling incest. This is an equally improper cultural translation of a very complex situation, to be considered later. At this point, however, it introduces the more familiar subject of the abrogation of the societal rule which prohibits such behavior among the less exalted members of the same society.[5] This relatively rare custom involves a consideration of an incest taboo in the original sense of the concept, since certain behavior is engaged in by prescription which is forbidden to others. This fact intimates the existence of cultural variability in a general comparative sense, and specifically refers to a deed of some magnitude, since it is hedged by ceremony and strict reservations.

The roll of royal incestuous societies can be rather extensive, but the commonly referred-to examples include the ruling families of archaic Egypt, Hawaii, Peru, and Thailand. More ambitious inquiries widen the scope to include a host of other centralized African societies, such as the Shilluk, Lovedu, Azande, and the Interlacustrine states, since incest is thematic for centralized governments on the continent. Comparative discussions, which attempt to account for this phenomenon, almost invariably assume that incestuous marriages are concurrently instances of inbreeding. Therefore the arguments attempt to account for royal incest in terms of the reproductive implications and consequences. Rarer inquiries into a single instance of royal incestuous marriage which do not inextricably link up marriage, sex, and reproduction have been more cautious in their eventual appraisal of the situation. The peculiar arrangement has not lacked for a response, and explanations for this form of incest often take flight from the same basic assumptions used to account for the prohibition. Specifically, the sociologically inclined glean the potential social functions of this arrangement, while sociobiologists see, not unexpectedly, biological profits. The former have been advancing their arguments for a longer time, but the latecomers have also had to tackle this very problem. Both have displayed some admirable ingenuity in proposing essentially flawed arguments.

For anthropologists recently converted to sociobiology, royal incest is seen as "a fitness maximizing strategy," derived from the "paradigm of inclusive fitness" (van den Berghe and Mesher 1980: 300). Stating the problem and solution in such a terminological fashion presents those who have adopted the new science of sociobiology with a definite advantage over their traditionally minded colleagues, less familiar with the genetic lexicon. Adopting a new scientific vocabulary is no failing if the facts under consideration are well grounded. However, if this is not the case, then it is only the illusion of a more rigorous science which replaces social science. There is no profit in such a conversion.

The sociobiological argument on the subject of royal incest presumes that reproduction by close kin has a deleterious effect on the offspring, due to the negative genetic consequences of inbreeding.[6] Despite the resistance of some social scientists, as seen, there is no reason to contend with this conclusion. The sociobiologists are also inclined to accept the Westermarck hypothesis regarding a universal aversion to sex at maturity by those raised in close physical proximity. Here, there is reason for some caution, since it is clear that this avoidance holds in some instances but not in others. Culture interjects itself in the form of domestic arrangements to either produce this avoidance or its antithesis in the form of sexual attraction. The particular response has to be demonstrated, rather than accepted as a given for every society.[7] In the case of royal domestic arrangements, relative unfamiliarity is probable for offspring, especially since they often have different mothers. Thus attraction is likely for the children of a royal household for the classic examples of royal incest. The historical or ethnographic evidence, however, is not uniform nor particular enough to allow for this conclusion with surety. In any event, royal incest would have to overcome one biological barrier and a possible psychosocial one to make sense. From a sociobiological perspective, the advantages of royal incest are not immediately obvious; but as the argument develops, some sense to the arrangement is perceived.

According to the proponents of a biological model for the interpretation of this arrangement, the female's benefit in mating with a royal full or half brother derives from her reproductive access to the highest-ranking male of her society. Status and, thus, optimal survival conditions of the children become the purported major considerations. This choice of the most dominant male by a woman for siring purposes is an example of the "fitness enhancing strategy" alluded to previously, since the offspring maintain the dominant social status of their mother. Because of her optimal position at the peak of the social system, any other form of marriage would involve mating with a lower-ranking male and a consequent loss of status for her children as they sank to his social level. Thus, for the highest-ranking female of the society, an incestuous marriage is the only solution to the problem of ensuring the maintenance or an increase in social dominance for her children. Other females of the group, whatever their status, are able to escape this dilemma, by resort to equal or even higher-ranking males available to them in the population, without having to resort to inbreeding. If carried to its reproductive conclusion, this behavior would have obvious biological implications affecting social status. However, such activity does not reflect the sexual patterns of lower primates, who, as noted, seek a nonrelated partner for mating, even if this entails loss of dominance for offspring. Thus this explanation points to a strong cultural impulse of this social strategy not available to other species. This implies that even according to this line of reasoning, incest is a human convention distinguishing our kind from other species.[8]

According to this approach, the social status of a female spouse is not a significant consideration for the royal male, since his legitimate offspring will inherit his position in society, as it is determined by his rank without serious reference to the mother's. The legitimate child of a king is royal, even if the mother is far removed from this rank. She is raised to this position by marriage. A fitness maximizing strategy therefore does not offer a relevant account for the male's participation in this rare arrangement. However, the notion of inclusive fitness, as the measure of an individual's genes in succeeding generations, is an important sociobiological consideration from the royal masculine viewpoint. According to this perspective, the male's chances of optimal achievement in this biological derby are enhanced by inbreeding, since reproduction with the sister results in a complete transfer of his genetic gifts to humanity in the next generation. The offspring of this union will be, as a consequence, a genetic replicant of the present ruler. This may not be a source of jubilation among the citizenry, but apparently this outcome is supposed to provide a modicum of royal satisfaction. Although marriage with a half sister, made possible by extensive royal polygyny in these societies, is more common, this arrangement still allows for a higher degree of inclusive fitness than if reproduction were achieved with a nonrelated female only.

Some may find it difficult to accept the premise that individual behavior, even among royalty, can be interpreted to any extent on these unfamiliar grounds. This is a reasonable and common enough reaction to sociobiological arguments, but there is no denying the outcome of royal incest as projected by the model. The child of such a union would achieve the unique elite status of the parents and also bear their genetic makeup to a peculiar degree. The sophisticated notions of fitness maximizing strategy and inclusiveness fitness are not intellectually suspect, but a simpler, if not the simplest, fact of life is debatable; that is, does the couple have offspring who would bear their social and biological imprint? The question is not concerned here with the morality or morbidity of progeny, for this is a recognized and natural concern of sociobiologists, who are generally more cognizant of this effect than social scientists. The issues are, instead, whether or not a marriage of this sort implies sex and, if so, does sex necessarily mean reproduction? Sociobiologists involved in the debate assume these facts of life, but others have shown their reticence to follow this lead by considering the historical and ethnographic evidence, rather than the sociobiological implications of the problem.

Sociobiologists were not the first to apply reputable scientific concepts and procedures to the elucidation of royal incest. The assumption has also been a time-honored notion of classicists and Egyptologists. Much earlier in the century, the distinguished British paleopathologist Sir Marc Ruffer (1921) turned his calipers and interest in ancient disease to the remains of royal Egypt. His measurements of length and width of trunk and limb, and cranial size, in comparison to the general characteristics of the population of the time, led Ruffer to wax effusively about the positive state of these royal mummies. His estimation of the historical record, in conjunction with his own novel scientific data, allowed him to conclude that there was no degeneration of mind or body, as well as no diminution of the ability to reproduce at a prolific pace for these presumed incestuous rulers. Indeed, according to Ruffer, both the males and females involved in these affairs of state were "fine, distinguished and handsome" (1921:335). This led him to suggest that for these royal specimens, at least, one could not detect any obvious negative effects of inbreeding which had been carried on for generations, spanning centuries.

However, earlier on in his presentation of the historical record, Ruffer interjected a cautionary note by remarking that, for the ancient Egyptians, the term "sister" was often employed as a euphemism for mistress, concubine, temporary wife (whatever that might have been), or even employed as a term of endearment for any female. He also mentions that the phrase "Royal Sister" was one of the queen's many official titles, regardless of her biological relationship to the Pharaoh (1921:324). This potential terminological confusion has also been noted by other students of classical Egyptian culture who have taken an interest in this peculiar conjugal arrangement, which eventually even reached down into the lower strata of society at the time. This proclivity of a male commoner to refer to his wife, even in the official written records, as "sister," though this was not the actual case, has resulted in the necessity to reduce the large number of apparent brother-sister marriages to a few involving half siblings (Cerney 1954:29).[9] Nonetheless, all the experts agree that full- or half-sibling marriage was a feature of ancient Egyptian society for both royalty and a proportion of commoners.[10] The questions of whether or not these relationships had a sexual and reproductive element and if, for the royalty, they were intended to or did produce an heir are distinct matters. These separate concerns are open to single consideration.

Challenging the common assumption of actual incest among Egyptian royalty, Bixler (1982a and 1982b) argues that, although the historical evidence for such marriages is undeniable, the same is not the case for sexual activity and especially for reproduction on the part of those involved. This bedeviling compression of different phenomena is characteristic, even for those who derive their explanations from biology. Bixler points out that the record is either unclear or in direct contradiction to the conclusion that incest, reproduction, and inheritance by offspring of high office followed from such marriages in the presumed classic examples of Egypt, Peru, Hawaii, and Thailand.[11] His review of the secondary sources by Egyptologists leads him to conclude that the assertion that the royalty of Egypt were an unbroken line of incestuous pairs is in fundamental error. Considering the data on the Ptolomeic line in particular, he notes that since the Pharaoh had so many wives, including his "sister," it is often not possible to determine the actual mother of the male child who succeeds and then marries his own sibling upon ascension to the Egyptian throne. Where the name of the successor's mother is known, he notes that in only one case was she identified as the Pharaoh's sister or half sister.

Bixler pays particular attention to the case of Cleopatra, the queen of textbook examples of incest. He explicitly notes that the records on Cleopatra VI indicate that not only was her father not a full-blooded descendant of the Ptolomies, but her mother was an unknown consort of the king, and likely a non-Egyptian Semite. Finally he mentions that although she married her two half brothers, both died before puberty under mysterious conditions which most historians lay to the political machinations of their ambitious sister (Bixler 1982a:271–272). In effect, Cleopatra had little love for her brothers in any sense of the word, and was much more concerned with her child by Caesar. If their child had come to the throne as Ptolomy XIV, he would not only have been untainted by incestuous blood, but he would also have had little, if any, royal or even Egyptian blood.[12] Since Cleopatra had "married" her brothers, no doubt some would have taken this result of extensive outbreeding as a final example of a long line of incestuous unions and indicating a lack of negative consequences.

The historical popularity of Cleopatra's romantic life, even in our times, intimates that such a projected conclusion may be unfair to suggest. However, there is no doubt that this whole matter of royal incest has been treated with little subtlety by most interested parties. Students of kingship, dynastic lines, and their claims of royal purity have long recognized that courtly behavior, even in the royal bedchamber, makes such ideological statements about parentage difficult to maintain in fact. The best the king and, for that matter, any male can ever hope for is that he is indeed the biological father of his heir. Male rulers, even in the rudest kingdoms, have long been aware of the problems involved in assuming paternity by jealously guarding the behavior of their consorts. This worldly attitude contrasts remarkably with the innocence of some scientists who have recently considered the intellectual problem of royal marriages. The concept of inclusive fitness provides sociobiology with an interesting explanation for why males tend to restrict the sexual behavior of the females they control while seeking to give their own reproductive capacity full expression. Unfortunately, despite its biological veracity in the realm of gene flow, inclusive fitness also rests upon some naive assumptions about human sexual behavior and fancy.

Maintaining a distinction among the concepts of sex, marriage, and reproduction, along with a modicum of common sense about human frailty, makes it unreasonable to assume that royal unions can be demystified by the notions of a fitness maximizing strategy and inclusiveness fitness. These refreshing and, in other instances, useful concepts are combined in this instance with an astonishing amount of innocence about human sexual behavior. The medley offers no solution to the problem of royal incest. Sociobiology makes infinitely more sense when it considers the absence of incest, for humans are then acting like other animals. However, when our species begins to act according to its unique capabilities, then biological reasoning is insufficient. When humans engage in, or portray, incest in social forms, it is far more profitable to consider the interpretation of social science. The initial failure of this approach to provide a complete explanation for incest prohibitions by relying exclusively on the importance of the concept of culture for inspiration has been referred to often enough. Thus there is justice in now balancing the scales. If incest is human, and therefore exclusively cultural, those who take an interest in human social activity should have more to offer than those who approach the problem from genetics and biology. In general this has been true, but the success rate has not been overwhelming. Many social scientists take a positivist view of human nature, and as a result too often emphasize the practical political consequences of royal marriages. An explanation for this arrangement on functional grounds is reasonable. However, at times it may be more useful to seek an understanding of a peculiar social custom, rather than to explain it away by reference to its consequences. A similar appreciation of the implications of the violation of the deed in the form of royal incest also has its limitations. If one sets out to find a function of some custom, the result is foregone. However, determining the consequences of some arrangement does not necessarily imply that the cause has been uncovered, nor does this approach signify that its cultural implications have been understood.

Although inherent to the definition of the problem, it is worth making explicit that these royal incestuous marriages are features of highly stratified economic, social, and political systems. Recognizing this, most commentators have sought the solution to the problem in the context of these status arrangements (Goggin and Sturtevant 1964). Some have suggested that, in view of their exalted position at the very apex of the society, the royal couple have only each other as suitable marriage partners. As reasonable as it seems, there are serious flaws to this explanation. For one, it considers the issue for one gender only, by ignoring the fact that the king has many other sexual partners, while this is not the case for the queen. The male's status is not affected by the rank of his wife, who becomes his equal by marriage, so this is not a crucial issue for him. Moreover, as mentioned, any legitimate child of a monarch is raised to the position of the father. The male, as royalty, need not be overly concerned with the social value of his spouse. In societies in which monogamy is the custom, this may be of some consideration, and thus more attention paid to the natal rank of the female spouse. Yet this factor is easily remedied by the choice of a female from the noble rank just below, who carries with her a trace of royal blood. The elevation to royalty is then merely a minor revision of the female's social station. In addition, the societies under consideration, especially classical Egypt, were not so isolated that a royal female could not be located in an adjacent society.

As suggested, this status argument overlooks the differing problem of a mate for a royal female. If she is not matched with a male of similar prestige from a neighboring state, then an available spouse of equal rank is precluded to her. Marriage to anyone other than a brother would entail at least some loss of status for herself and her offspring. Furthermore, this would be her only marriage partner, since only males in these societies can have more than one legitimate partner at the same time. Her offspring would not be royalty, yet they would be descended directly from this office through their mother's father, who was a previous ruler. Presuming that marriage for the royal sister would also be with an aristocratic male closely related to the reigning line would mean that the child of the union could also trace descent through his father to the throne. This outcome points to a different possible function value of royal brother-sister marriage, formerly overlooked by commentators.

A royal sister who is not wed to her brother could nonetheless produce a child with an alternate claim to a throne. Usurpation by such a branch would have a strong claim to royal legitimacy. However, if the royal sister is precluded from marrying anyone but her brother, then this potentiality is avoided. If such a union is devoid of sex and reproduction, and the latter seems to be the case most often, then she is rendered socially sterile by this peculiar royal custom. The "incestuous" relationship in effect neutralizes the sister, who becomes a pawn, rather than queen. In sum, royal brother-sister marriage may not intend to determine a suitable spouse and produce socially agreeable children, but may, in contrast, result in a prevention of the sister from reproducing legitimate offspring. Such a consideration also renders suspect the related argument that incestuous marriages aim at producing a royally pure heir to the throne. The historical facts do not bear out such fertility as a political pattern. This arrangement does not preclude sexual relations between the royal siblings, nor between the sister and other men, especially if she is married in name only to her brother. But as she is allowed only one spouse, the latter alternative would entail adultery, and reproduction would be a politically dangerous affair.

This analysis is not offered as a total sociological solution to the complex matter of royal incest. However, the social logic does make some sense, since these marriages cannot be demonstrated to have the reproductive effect commonly assumed. Indeed, they seem to have the opposite value, and a reasonable functional argument should address the outcome of a social arrangement, which in this case is the patterned absence of the reproduction of an heir. This lack of reproduction has some practical value for the male involved, and could also be interpreted as reducing the potential for political conflict for society at large, since it minimizes alternate claims to the throne. A functional estimation of royal incestuous marriages might well consider these implications of the curious custom. This contrasting interpretation of the problem also indicates, as suggested earlier, that if a function of arrangement is sought, then there will be no difficulty in eliciting a defensible one, even if it is in direct contradiction to prevailing conclusions. Unless we presume that humans generate customs only for the sake of solutions to potential social problems, then there is good reason to continue to explore this cultural curiosity. The imagery of an incestuous conjugal bed · serves to generate some rather fertile ideas about the nature of kingship, having little directly to do with practical political affairs. The less mundane implications of these forbidden marriages have also drawn their share of commentary.

The world of incestuous kings is often conceived of as a heavenly realm. The figures involved are expected to engage in behavior suitable only to gods on earth. This complicated notion of deity and humanity as one does not in itself offer an explanation for their incestuous behavior.[13] Recognition of royal deification merely reflects a richer aspect of what is often involved when rulers are asked to emulate their mythical ancestors, and in the process contravene the standards which govern the mortals they lead. Defining the problem in this cultural fashion suggests that political ideology and related notions of divinity are more relevant than political strategy and biology. If we wish to understand what is at issue when royal incest is enjoined, in contrast to predicting the outcome of the arrangement, then these matters deserve equal consideration, if not precedence. For political rulers, incest is hardly a practical concern revolving around succession to the throne. In the perceptive words of one student of royalty, incest is the "primordial sin of kings and queens" (Yamaguchi 1972:47). The crucial issue becomes one of determining why such individuals are required to commit, and tempt the consequences of, this grievous sin, rather than assuming that they revel in a salacious freedom denied to others. As Shakespeare suggests, "nice customs curtsy to great kings," but his world of kings is also tragic.

As the result of a lifelong study of traditional royalty in Central Africa, Luc de Heusch has raised the level of our appreciation of royal incest.[14] Noting that incestuous marriages and the sacralization of the leader go hand in hand, he argues that the custom is a powerful symbol of the emergence of a new political order. The centralization of authority the incestuous union presupposes indicates that the old political order, based upon the rules of a kinship-based society, are no longer relevant. As a divinity, the political leader in such polities takes no cognizance of kinship relations by engaging in incest. By flaunting this rule, which governs all others, the king's incestuous marriage indicates that he has no kinsmen. This stands in contrast to the behavior of others in this regard, which is hedged by a variety of regulations. Projected by this forbidden act into a realm of "incestuous solitude" (de Heusch 1981: 102) at the summit of society, the king is representative of an individual belonging to no kinship group. In such societies, this renders royalty as nonhuman. At the same time, this union, in con-

junction with his many other marital alliances, ties him to all kinship groups in society. Thus the king is simultaneously the most
alienated and related of individuals, which places him at the center
of the social system. He is the most social and antisocial of human
beings, and as such the epitome of both divinity and humanity. He
is a living paradox of social life, a god on earth.

This definition of his station also reconciles centralized authority
with the presumption of social justice, since the king is equally related by marriage to all and by descent to none. All men are equal
before him. On the other hand, his nonhuman status and deification, exemplified by this deed of incest, legitimizes the typical tyr-
anny of centralized political systems. However, a reign of terror is
also a democracy in that it recognizes no favorites. As de Heusch
suggests, the societies which adjusted to divine kingship were at
least dimly aware that "they were playing with fire" (de Heusch
1981:25). They may conjure up from among their own the wrath of
god, and often a holy terror. This is not always the case, but it is
more certain that for traditional political systems, incest, by its inversion of the social order, heralds the appearance of other new conventions.

The divine queenship of the Lovedu of southeastern Africa, which
is one of the continent's most striking cultural anomalies, lends further support to the idea that sanctioned incest presages the emergence of a new social order. According to their traditions, their state
was founded by the son of a brother-sister marriage, who fled to a
new land. In subsequent generations, they were ruled over by a succession of nonincestuous kings descended from these siblings. However, at one point in their history, the Lovedu were beset by a series
of natural and civil disorders. Tradition states that the reigning king
attempted to negate these misfortunes by incest with his daughter,
for the deed harks back to the original beneficial state of Lovedu
affairs. With this inversion of the moral and social orders, the father
and daughter sought to generate a new beginning for society. The
male child first born of this illicit union subsequently died, suggesting that the prevailing disasters would not be eliminated by the traditional pattern of male succession and leadership. The second
child, as a female, offered a more propitious omen of future tranquility, since her elevation to the throne would in itself contradict

the existing political system beset by strife, external threat, and natural calamity. These reversals of fortune were overcome with her succession and the establishment of female precedence. Since then the queens, who still reign to this day, have served as the guarantors of a harmonious social order. Their actual political power is virtually nonexistent, as males exercise authority in their name. However, the queen's symbolic role as the representative of society and the foe of chaos remains undiminished.[15]

Contemporary arrangements among these people also contain a hint of royal incest, since the successor to the throne is said to be a daughter of the queen and a half brother. However, the behavior of the queen is secluded from the public gaze, and the ancestry of the monarch is a closely guarded secret (Krige 1975).[16] The situation is further complicated by the fact that the queen herself has numerous "wives." These virginal females are provided to her by local-level chiefs from their female kin, since the queen's wife is a position of great status. The women of the royal household are the official wives of the queen, but they may become pregnant by her brothers and other closely related male kin. What is significant about this custom is that the daughters of this arrangement are also candidates for the queenship, since their official "husband" is the queen.

All this suggests quite firmly that in their mating behavior Lovedu political figures show little concern for the sociobiological strategies alluded to earlier.[17] Moreover, the kinship relations between the principal figures involved reflect social, rather than biological, patterns. The queen in particular is a symbolic figure, and her behavior accords well with this cultural definition. Her major responsibilities include insuring rainfall for a successful harvest and warding off external threats to the kingdom by her control over these natural forces, which, it is believed, could be brought to bear against the enemies of the state. Producing a royal heir and finding a suitable husband are not major concerns. These mundane considerations may be the cares of ordinary mortals, but not of a divinity. Classic sociological interpretations, or newly minted biological ones fixating on the functional consequences of royal incest, unjustly sweep away these crucial cultural factors. The theme of incest, which attaches itself in prominent fashion to the myth, history, and traditional political system of the Lovedu and other centralized states of Africa and other parts of the world, is indicative of the power of this incestuous idea to legitimize the emergence of a society in its particular form.

The presumption of the indulgence in the deed as an idea concerned with the ability to create and recreate society from a single social atom is convincingly argued by Leach, in his provocative analysis of incest in the Bible.[18] In a distinctly nontheological approach to a sacred Western text, Leach points out that the stories about the sibling-like Adam and Eve in the Garden of Eden, Noah and his sons after the flood, and Lot and his daughters after the destruction of Sodom all contain hints or explicit reference to incest by the participants. In each instance, society is either nonexistent, as in Eden, or has to be reestablished in response to the destructive power of the Creator. Thus, by resort to incest, Leach argues, these humans share with divinity the capacity to create society from a vacuum or chaos. Leach's insights draw attention to a potentially universal theme of creation stories and add another interpretative dimension to the behavior of royalty involved in incestuous arrangements. In those societies in which the monarchs are deemed a reflection of divinity, their responsibility to create the social order is shared with this vital force. From this perspective, it is not surprising that the act implied is a sexual one—an exercise in the creation of form. This elemental power of regal incest deserves further elaboration, for the arrangement returns literal meaning to the term "omnipotent."

The rejection of sociobiology and, to a lesser extent, familiar sociological commentary on royal incestuous marriages in favor of what is interpreted as a cultural drama by society's main actors is not prejudicial. The custom of brother-sister marriage among commoners in Roman Egypt is, as already noted, a unique and vexing issue. The individuals involved in this instance seem to have been serving their own interests, rather than society's. The implications of their behavior not only point to the variability of human culture, but also to the potential value of sociological analysis, concerned with strategic choices for inheritance and maintenance of a family estate. This was a propertied segment of the population living under foreign domination, which involved the imposition of alien laws and taxation. This situation of the middle class in any age or place demands a social-historical inquiry, but not so for the behavior of kings, who are often perceived as gods on earth. Their problems and responsibilities are quite different. The world of kings is an enigmatic one. Understanding the realm requires grappling with both magistery and mystery.

CHAPTER 8

The Power
of Incest (I)

To be a god does not necessarily mean to have more
license, but rather to have more duties: *divinité
oblige*.   HOCART, 1970

THE PRECEDING CHAPTER argued that royal incest involves form
rather than substance. As such, the custom draws attention to actors engaged in cultural performance rather than reproductive strategy. This definition of the situation suggests that neither the canons
of sociobiology nor functional analysis is useful in unraveling the
complexities. The interpretation briefly advanced in their stead focused on the potential cultural content of an often symbolic alliance between two individuals denied to the masses. This dream of
the forbidden becomes the center of public attention. Although this
relationship also implies the possibility of a sexual act and reproduction, it makes little if any difference if one or both actually take
place. A profound cultural message is transmitted by the mere hint
of an otherwise forbidden sexual relationship. As a result, understanding the meaning of both the symbolized incestuous relationship and the deed requires something more than a glancing appreciation of the culture.

In addition to being a feature of human culture in a broad sense,
incest, in the form of an institutionalized relationship in a particular society, has the responsibility of transmitting specific cultural
messages. Understanding these calls for an appreciation of the encompassing system of meaning, customs, and institutions. Consequently there are rewards in considering in some detail a society

with a flourishing divine kingship reflecting the expected implication of royal incest. This inkling of the forbidden takes place at a moment of societal crises, for the incestuous drama is embedded in the procedure for the installation of a new king after the demise of an incumbent. Thus the ritual process is concerned not only with turning a noble into a king, but also with transforming a human being into a deity. The one permutation is a complex enough cultural feat in redefinition, while the combination of the two requires some rather elaborate ceremonial. The theme of incest plays a major part in the deification procedure, for its reflects the ability of the would-be king to violate a basic rule and survive the encounter with a symbolic act of potency and creation.

The people in question are the Shilluk of the southern Sudan, who to this day are ruled over by a divine king referred to as the *reth*. Despite the fact that they have never been properly studied by an anthropologist, or possibly because of this absence of an authority, they have always been one of anthropology's favorite societies, open to commentary by all and sundry.[1] This academic attraction has also been due in no small part to a Western fascination with their peculiar political system, headed by a man-god, which evokes such mysterious images of the continent. This vision of the divine king of nineteenth-century Africa, in conjunction with romantic sketches of the same figure from our classical past, led Sir James Frazer to portray this institution in the opening page of his celebrated *The Golden Bough*. He wrote, in lines which bear repeating:

> Who does not know Turner's picture of the Golden Bough. . . . In antiquity this sylvan landscape was the scene of a strange and recurring tragedy. . . . In this sacred grove there grew a certain tree round which at any time of the day, and probably far into the night, a grim figure might be seen to prowl. In his hand he carried a drawn sword, and he kept peering warily about him as if at every instant he expected to be set upon by an enemy. He was a priest and a murderer, and the man for whom he looked was sooner or later to murder him and hold the priesthood in his stead. . . .
>
> The post which he held by this precarious tenure carried with it the title of king; but surely no crowned head ever lay

uneasier, or was visited by more evil dreams, than his. For
year in and year out, in summer and winter, in fair weather
and in foul, he had to keep his lonely watch, and whenever
he snatched a troubled slumber it was at the peril of his life.
The least relaxation of his vigilance, the smallest abatement
of his strength of limb or skill of fence, put him in jeopardy;
grey hairs might seal his death-warrant. To gentle and pious
pilgrims at the shrine, the sight of him might well seem to
darken the fair landscape, as when a cloud suddenly blots the
sun on a bright day (1963:1).

The style of academic writing has clearly suffered since Frazer's
time. Grand questions about the meaning of existence are also no
longer fashionable, but divine kingship, and even the isolated
Shilluk as its cultural paradigm, has commanded continued attention. Their location along the White Nile, just south of the Arab-
Islamic culture zone, meant that they are encountered in the European explorer literature earlier and with greater frequency than
many neighboring sub-Saharan peoples. As an example, in the 1760s,
while in the northern Sudan in search of the source of the Nile, the
Scottish explorer James Bruce (1905) mentions the Shilluk in passing as a pagan people somewhere to the south, ruled over by a fa-
mous king said to be put to death by his subjects or a usurper when
he became aged, infirmed, or careless of his personal safety. Unfortunately, there is only this tantalizing reference to the situation,
since Bruce then struck east along the course of the Blue Nile,
which took him into Ethiopia. Nonetheless, his few words drew
attention to Shilluk kings and their unusual demise. These romantic
figures provided continued fascination to others of Bruce's ilk and
then later to the inevitable missionaries on their civilizing mission.[2]

More in our time, interested academics have disputed the nature
of Shilluk kingship, with regard to the actual political authority of
the officeholder and the method of his departure from his earthly
realm. Some have suggested he was an all-powerful tyrant, while
others argued in contrast that he was merely a politically impotent
figurehead, a slave to customary restrictions on his behavior im-
posed by those who looked upon him as a deity.[3] Stories were
bandied about that he was smothered in his sleep when old or ill
by his senior wife, walled up toward the end of his days with a

favorite, or, alternately, slain in the night by an ambitious pretender to the throne. These compelling images transported the classic grove of the ancient goddess Diana at Nemi to the contemporary shores of the Nile in Africa.

Whatever the historical truth of the matter, it is safe to say that the Shilluk continue to state that as a deity the *reth* may not, and does not, die like other mortals. Even today they maintain that his passage to his other realm is made possible by helping hands, if only during his last moments. As the animate symbol of their existence, if he were to succumb to the forces of entropy in the form of a natural death, the same fate would be in store for their society. His primary symbolic function calls for the control over natural forces, so that his unassisted demise as the consequence of these very powers would indicate a supreme failure, boding ill for his subjects.

In sum, Shilluk society and culture reflects a regnal idiom. The passing seasons, years, and important events are marked in terms of the kingship. This institution informs the Shilluk interpretation of time and space, and gives ultimate meaning to their existence on earth. The office and its holder form the center point of their cosmology from which all other things radiate. Whatever the initial concern, it is eventually given added substance by reference to kingship and its properties. The office, through its temporary incumbent, who is raised to deity, brings the rain which insures a satisfactory crop in a precarious environment competed against with only a simple technology. The *reth's* office also insures against external political threats and maintains the internal order by adjudicating major disputes. Thus he is their society, in the sense of the symbolic integration of natural, social, and supernatural forces. All spheres of human experience are one and at peace with him. Given all of this, what happens when—as he must, for he is human as well as divine—he meets his end? The demise and actual decomposition of the body politic before their very eyes is not a matter to be taken casually by a people committed to such a vision of society.[4] A simple leave-taking would be insufficient, nor is this the case. Both death and rebirth have to be attended to with a flourish in this cultural setting. An appreciation of what transpires at this moment depends upon additional information on Shilluk social organization and traditions, which take them back to the very beginnings of historical times only a few centuries ago.

The Shilluk, who now number about two hundred thousand living in a series of agricultural hamlets strung along the western banks of the Nile for 110 miles, were led into their present homeland from somewhere farther south by Nyikang, their first king and culture hero. Upon arrival, he and a band of followers encountered the original inhabitants of the area, who were subdued and incorporated into the polity, and their descendants remain a distinct group to the present. In the process of conquest and consolidation, Nyikang meted out large sections of the country to his followers for administration. These in turn appointed others at a lower level as headmen of local communities. Nyikang succeded in this and other admirable political feats before, as the Shilluk say, he "blew away" and was replaced by his son. As a god and founder of society, Nyikang could not die. This spectacular disappearance took place in the northernmost part of their country, which is closely associated with his continued spiritual essence and contains the most important shrine in his honor. This memorial houses his spiritual presence, for his departure allowed for no physical remains. However, the person of Nyikang is represented by an effigy of straw, ostrich feathers, and cloth, carefully draped over a pole. This unspectacular collection of common enough items remains inactive until the death of one of Nyikang's successors and the installation of another, who will absorb their powerful spiritual essence and thus unite the country under his banner.

The aforementioned political divisions, each led by a chief, are in turn grouped together to form two overarching provinces, representing what is primarily a ritual dichotomy of the country into northern and southern halves. The physical boundary between the two major territorial sections is a minor watercourse located just south of Fashoda, the ceremonial capital and geographical center of the country. Each half of Shillukland is represented in ritual matters by one of the division chiefs. The hereditary leader of the district just to the south of Fashoda occupies one such position, while his counterpart from the immediate northern one occupies the other. This structural system of territorial oppositions culminates in the kingship, associated, as noted, with the very center of the country.

In addition to these territorial arrangements, the Shilluk are also stratified by social considerations reflecting the political hierarchy. The greater segment of the population is grouped into numerous clans, referred to as *colo*, which is also a variation on the Shilluk name for themselves. Distinguished from this mass are the *ororo*, a particular clan descended from a previous king who brought disaster to the country by his political incompetence. Although his descendants no longer have a royal claim, as former royalty they take a major responsibility for burying a deceased king. Their association with the danger and pollution of death means the *ororo* women are avoided as marriage partners of the monarch. Since the *reth* will effect an incestuous marriage bond with his paternal half sister, who is a member of his own clan, the *ororo* are the only group with whom he does not establish a marital alliance. However, since they attend him at his death, ironically they are his final partners and thus no group in society escapes an intimate connection to the throne.

Continuing up the social hierarchy, one encounters the *kwareth*, the numerous members of the royal clan claiming descent from any previous king. These are followed in order by the *bang reth*, the personal retainers of a reigning monarch, who earn personal prestige by their connection to the throne. Those counted among this group serve the king in various capacities during his reign. After his death, they and their descendants maintain his burial shrine, located in the particular geographical area he emerged from and ruled. Thus the Shilluk countryside is dotted with shrines to former divine rulers and associated villages of former retainers keeping the personal faith.

Finally, at the apex of the social system stands the *reth* himself, a figure of enormous prestige and the object of exceptional deference by those who count themselves fortunate enough to bask in his presence even momentarily, in the quest for favor or blessing. He is surrounded by intermediaries, and his personal behavior is equally circumscribed by taboos of all sorts. These include being shielded from those who have been in contact with illness, death, menstruating females, pregnant women, and those who have recently given birth. As a consequence women, except for a portion of his many wives, are virtually excluded from his presence. Men also find it difficult to gain an audience. The fear of assassination, today more of a historical notion than a real threat, is deferred to by appropriate secretive behavior. Thus, according to this regal performance, his movements, and particularly his nocturnal resting-place, are known in advance to only a few. When he travels about his realm by government transport—during the colonial days on a great white donkey, and in the present by Land Rover—he is accompanied by armed guards, who invariably fire a round or two to announce the presence of deity among the locals. A personal bugler indicates the same in a discordant tune. Women and children know enough to scatter at his arrival, while the fortunate adult males must take to the ground and heap dust upon head and body until commanded to rise to their knees.

In his dual capacity as the shining apex of the political and social hierarchy, the *reth* of the Shilluk has been referred to since Frazer's time as the classic instance of an extant "divine kingship." This is a vaguely defined and disputed type of centralized political system which has drawn its share of academic controversy.[5] Moreover, there has been some debate over this particular example, centering on the actual secular power of the officeholder, since he is primarily defined in the local context as a sacred figure. Nonetheless, the *reth* is an undisputed cultural symbol, since, as remarked, the institution informs the Shilluk experience of the past and present in a variety of significant contexts. This position is, as often mentioned, the center of their cosmological system. This importance of the office to a Shilluk understanding of existence is of primary concern here.

The Shilluk, as with neighboring groups, conceive of the divinity as able to represent itself simultaneously in a number of different forms and contexts while at the same time remaining a single entity. The Christian theological notion of the Trinity is an instructive parallel, as it also allows for the divinity to be expressed in various guises and realms as Father, Son, and Holy Ghost without diminishing among the faithful the idea of a single God and Creator. Admittedly, this is a mystery, but then this perplexity is an essential feature of religion. The Shilluk, with their god in heaven and on earth, maintain the same enigma.

In one sense the Shilluk central cosmological figure, referred to as *Juok*, as an immanent being, created the universe and its first humans and animals at some unspecified point in a land distant from their present homeland. A domestic dispute in their Garden of Eden resulted in a portion of the second generation of human beings, which included Nyikang, to set out to create a new society in the external world, ushering in a new era. Defined in this distant spatial and temporal context, *Juok* recedes from Shilluk experience. In this removed capacity as the creator of original time and space, this aspect of divinity, though powerful and extant, diminishes in practical importance. Thus *Juok* plays little part in Shilluk daily religious activities. This force in human affairs is replaced by Nyikang, one of his earliest creations. By his feats, Nyikang is responsible for the creation and order of Shilluk society as now experienced. As the originator of the social order, Nyikang, their first ruler and reflection of the divinity formerly among them in historical time, becomes a more immanent and approachable figure. He is resorted to in prayer and ritual by the Shilluk in daily activities as "god below" (*juok piny*). Each successive king becomes one with Nyikang at his installation; and as the living representation of divinity, each ruler assumes the responsibility of being the living guarantor of society by his physical presence. The king and society are one, while his vitality and goodwill are essential to Shilluk continuity. With him there is order, and without him, chaos.

In this sense the *reth* of these people reigns as a divine king. From this perspective, religion is concerned with mediating between an omnipotent god in heaven and impotent man on earth (Leach and Aycock 1983:67). This Shilluk theological construct takes form and function with the presence and activities of the ruler, who is both man and god. His behavior transports the presence of divinity into their daily lives, and without him they are separate from this realm and lost. His death thus evokes the potential for the dissolution and eventual decay of the Shilluk cosmos in a single stroke of disaster, for, according to them, at this moment "there is no land." The creation of a new *reth* is at the same time the recreation of a failing universe. This implies that the successor to the throne must ritually demonstrate during the installation process his power to revive the land with his physical capacities and, in doing so, occupy the central position of the Shilluk cosmos. He must become one with the people and the divinity and, as such, cease to exist as a separate entity. As the Shilluk representative of their elective body put it when he informs a candidate that he is their choice for elevation: "You are our slave. We want to kill you."

The royal incestuous episode, which can now be interpreted in the context of a particular people's political arrangements, world view, and ritual system, takes place during the course of an elaborate and drawn-out installation ceremony, set in motion by the demise of the prior incumbent some months before. The death and burial of one ruler and the installation of another involve overlapping phases of a single and continuous ritual process. Interspersed are contrasting moments of ritual concern for the deceased king and the living candidate who, although nominated, has yet to achieve divine status. The mortuary stage for the one is as extensive as the installation procedure for the other, but only a few features of the former need be noted in order to grasp the essential messages concerned with the symbolic analogy between the person of the ruler and the state itself as inseparable entities.[6]

When the end of his days are judged near, the reigning officeholder is taken by his retainers from his personal residence to Fashoda, the official capital of the land. If they have been too late to make such arrangements, the body is transported there by members of the *ororo* clan, as the royal undertakers. Although his passing becomes public knowledge, there is no sign of personal or public mourning. His spirit, which is supposed to be assisted in leaving the body by ritual regicide, is that of Nyikang, and it departs to take up residence in the latter's effigy at his major shrine in the northern extremity of Shillukland. Here it will remain until its journey to the capital to enter the body of the successor at the moment of enthronement. Thus, whatever happens to its human temple, the essence of the Shilluk divinity on earth remains extant, for society cannot exist without its presence. At this point a successor is named. After the deceased has been removed from the capital, the elected takes up residence there under close guard, for traditionally passed-over claimants to the throne are apt to resort to violence at this time. He remains in seclusion at the center of the land, while the former *reth* is laid to rest and preparations begin for the installation to take place in a few months' time.

These carefully allotted activities include the procurement or construction of items such as ivory, skins, spears, fans, cloth, and precious metals by traditionally assigned territorial groups, so that each segment of society plays a role in "constructing" a king to rule over all. A particular group has the responsibility for providing a virginal young girl as a new bride for the monarch, who will play a crucial role in contrasting the purity and vitality of life with the pollution and decay of death. When all has been made ready, the installation process begins in earnest. The candidate and his entourage are informed by the masters of ceremony that the effigies of Nyikang and his son have left their northern shrine and are approaching Fashoda with numerous supporters from this half of the country to test his claim to the throne. With this initial movement of a spiritual force from north to south, the nominated begins to experience a series of spiritually dangerous confrontations, which are to transform him into a deity by proving his mettle during these encounters.

After a few days of desultory travel through the countryside, picking up further physical support, this collection camps just north of the capital. Here they prepare to do stylized battle with the candidate and his supporters, who have gathered from the south. Upon learning that the northerners have reached this point, the central figure in this ceremonial drama retreats from the rise at Fashoda southward to a nearby village, where his own forces are encamped. Here, at this designated moment in time, he spends the night in privacy with his half sister, in a violation of Shilluk sexual regulations. Although others who have commented on this incident suggest that sexual activity actually takes place, this cannot be confirmed.[7] All we know is that the royal pair are alone for this period. This nocturnal proximity is sufficient to symbolize the act of incest designated by the Shilluk as *dwalo*, a concept implying misfortune or disease. The half-sibling pair are not ritually married, nor is there any contemporary or historical evidence of ensuing reproduction. Thus it is best to view the Shilluk, and likely many others counted in this fashion, as symbolic instances of incestuous royalty.

The chosen female is of course forbidden to marry, as are all the other sisters and half sisters of the ruler. As noted, this is a common feature of these arrangements. Thus this form of pseudoincest exemplifies the counterclaim to the idea of inclusive fitness, since the female's genetic makeup, which is similar to that of the monarch, is prevented from being transmitted to the next generation by social conventions. Clearly, this incestuous liaison is intended to make a cultural statement about the ability of a chosen individual to violate rules and survive the experience, rather than to attempt to reproduce with a genetically similar mate. As evidence of this proposition, all other Shilluk males who have committed some sexual delict during their lifetimes also gather at this incestuous site. In the morning, the candidate's first act is to confront these other men and absolve them of their guilt by relieving them of their sins. With these two acts, he is well on his way toward achieving a divine status; but other trials await him.

Having demonstrated his newly acquired divine powers, the claimant gathers his force of sinners from the south to confront the divine spirit of goodness from the north. He recrosses the stream which separates them at Fashoda, and the two sides engage in a mock but physical melee, involving the exchange of thrown grain stalks and stick fights at the base of the rise at the capital. According to form, the candidate and his supporters lose this contest, and he is taken prisoner by the army of Nyikang, along with the pure young girl who accompanied him into battle. In this role of a prisoner of Nyikang, he is escorted up the hill at Fashoda, to another major shrine to the deity, where the seat of kingship awaits. First, the effigy is placed on the stool and removed; then the about-to-be king takes its place. In replacing the effigy, he visibly shudders as the spirit of divinity enters his body. Having now been fused with the spirit of the creator, he is finally the *reth* and god below, though still a prisoner of the effigy. More exploits reflecting his newfound prowess must be demonstrated.

He spends the first evening of his reign at the capital, this time in the company of three *ororo* women who, as mentioned, belong to a clan associated with the stigmata of historical failure and the pollution of death, which he has been shielded from since his nomination. This second sexual encounter contains a further hint of incest, since the king is related to these women through a common distant ancestor. This forbidden liaison not only implies incest, but also envelops the notions of death and failure and thus demands that the new *reth* confront other dangerous elements of the Shilluk cultural universe.

On the following morning, he emerges from the presence of these women to lead his troops in a second clash with the forces of the effigy at the same spot as the previous one. As the vessel of the divinity in this instance, and the conqueror of death, failure, and sexual pollution, not surprisingly he and his entourage now overcome the opposition. He then reclaims the maiden lost in the first battle and returns to the rise in triumph, with her and the effigy in tow. The effigy of divinity makes a final subservient appearance and is returned to its shrine from whence it came, to await the death of the new king. Thus in one sense the spirit of Nyikang is always the victor. The next phase of the installation procedure involves secular events initiating the political reign of the new king, as he receives the advice and obsequences of the district chiefs. In turn, he demands they locate and return any missing cattle or other goods of his predecessor which are now his. The latter requests indicate that the king is human as well as divine.

As to the symbolic significance of these activities, which stress the theme of incest, there are a number of now obvious interpretations. Among these are, first, recognizing that the liminal or transitional stage of the installation ceremony, when the candidate emerges from seclusion to be transformed into a divinity before assuming his public political function, involves him in a series of conjunctions with categories normally kept apart in Shilluk cosmology. These include (1) the merger of the geographically opposed halves of the country, with the melees at the center of the capitol; (2) the joining of the secular and sacred domains respectively represented by the candidate and effigy, which are figuratively fused at the moment of enthronement; (3) the physical coming together of the half siblings, either sexually or not, in contradiction to the prohibition on such contact between close relatives; and (4) the second purported incestuous sexual encounter between the male candidate, who is to stand for the triumvirate of vitality, success, and order, with women representing death, failure, and decay. In each instance, the claimant succeeds in these encounters, and in doing so validates his nomination to the Shilluk throne.

The symbolic implications of these particular activities are now standard anthropological fare and readily appreciated as the consequence of Beidelman's (1966) pioneering analysis of African royal ritual. In this convincing schema, he proposes that employing the notion of "cosmetics," in the sense of making something orderly, is essential to an understanding of these national occasions of king-making. Royal rites, Beidelman argues, "involve a dangerous but potent process of increasing animation, a combination of various symbolic attributes (in terms of the king) not normally together" (1966:389). The Shilluk material just considered, from another part of Africa, also directs the candidate for kingship to enter into contexts of social and cultural centrality. The would-be king must occupy and survive personal encounters fixed at the center of social relationships, even if they be forbidden ones and thus dangerous to experience.

However, the second major integral and recurring theme of the installation ceremony, which draws attention to sexual activity, rather than the cosmological structure of the events, deserves equal attention. The acts alluded to in this context involve, in turn, the normally illicit sexuality of the candidate with a prohibited, closely related female, followed by a similar liaison with three women more distantly related but nonetheless forbidden to him. This is followed by his reunion with a virginal and nonrelated sexual partner free of any social, cultural, or historical taint. Thus the principal figure is initially engaged in a forbidden sexual relationship, which sets in motion the crucial stage of installation. This ceremonial phase also entails a more distant incestuous encounter, and finally a permissible arrangement, which brings to a close the ritual process. Thus his sexual activity in the context of differing social relationships, ranging from the forbidden to the ideal, punctuates the installation ceremony.

Admittedly, it is mechanical and at least somewhat arbitrary to impose interpretive divisions on an integrated ritual process by imposing the three distinct stages of separation, transition, and incorporation (see Van Gennep 1960 and Turner 1962). However, it does seem reasonable to adopt this lead in the interpretation of the sexual element of Shilluk installation. The first two liaisons, incestuous in nature, indicate the transitional or liminal ritual stage designed to redefine the status of the participant. Normally, an individual who undergoes such a rite of passage emerges with a redefined social position shared with other members of society. In the case of

Shilluk installation, the intent is to eradicate the previous social identity and to create a unique cultural being, a divinity on earth. In this instance, the candidate for divine kingship encounters a ritualized situation, implying the loss of social identity by a presumed act, which fails to heed the existence of social divisions which define permissible and nonpermissible sexual partners. In one sense of its interpretation, incest does not recognize the existence of society in the form of constituent groups, so that the individual who engages in such behavior has no social identity. Incest denies the crucial human distinction between We and They, which binds the perception and behavior of other beings.

This loss of a social identity is achieved by a physical act Leach (1976:62) characterizes as one in which the sensory distinction between self and other is lost, so that the individual, momentarily at least, ceases to exist as a separate entity. Therefore it may not be too outlandish to suggest that the Shilluk achieve their cultural goal of god- and king-making by placing their candidate in a situation by which, metamorphically, he becomes one with the universe, as opposed to one or any of its parts. He becomes society itself, rather than a member of such a concept. This unique definition of an individual is achieved in a context implying physical creation, evoking a return to the beginning of social time and the absence of rules. In effect, the Shilluk have been returned to the era of Nyikang, who initially created their society from a void. Each new king must therefore engage in recreating and becoming the essence of society, which has failed with the death of an incumbent.

From the Shilluk perspective, these ritualized encounters, entailing as they do the abrogation of basic social rules usually associated with subsequent disaster for the individual involved, illuminate the candidate's ability to survive danger. As noted, this is in itself a validation of office. However, in contrast to the more typical rite of passage, where an initiate passively confronts the danger deriving from the loss of previous identity, the protagonist in this case actively creates this jeopardy with his own person and capabilities. In effect, the candidate further demonstrates his power to rule by not only overcoming perilous situations for ordinary mortals, but in addition by creating them with his actions. This capacity to create and overcome danger befits the definition of an office which implies divinity. Finally, his reseizure of the virginal girl, who is neither the source of pollution nor related to him, signals the end of the transitional period of the ritual. At this point the candidate, now king, displays his humanity with acceptable social behavior, since he is both man and god.

A key element in the ritual is the notion of power, which in Western political thought is normally restricted as a concept to the secular ability to control the actions of others. However, in the political system considered here, such a capability is severely restricted. The relevant demonstration of power is a supernatural exercise in creation. Thus the king's political legitimacy is "charismatic" in nature. This Weberian (1968) concept, originally concerned with the recognition of the right to rule, has in our time suffered from general usage by its application to inconsequential contexts. In the process it has been reduced to a vague psychological capacity of a popular figure. Weber's initial concern, however, was with defining the social setting which prompted the masses to recognize the "transcendency" of a particular individual. For latter-day interpreters of Weber, this would involve not only popular appeal, but the ability of an individual to prove himself by personal experience. This phenomenon implies significant cultural performances at the recognized heart of the social system.[8]

The psychological component of charisma derives, then, from an individual's encounter with existing social forms and conventions. Personality must be demonstrated in significant contexts. Moreover, these charismatic cultural performances are often contrary to social norms and experience. An individual is politically legitimized by challenging existing behavior and morality, since charisma is also a prominent assault on the sacred and a denial of propriety (Eisenstadt 1968). Charisma is thus essentially antisocial. Accordingly, a display of charismatic fervor has the added quality of defining society by drawing attention to its moral limits. At the same time, the reflector of charisma is redefined by the breach of these strictures. The royal incestuous episodes of the Shilluk convey both the psychological and social aspects of charisma, for both society and an individual have been created in the ritual process of king-making. In this sense, charisma is displayed, in Geertz's words, as ". . . a sign, not of popular appeal of inventive craziness, but of being near the heart of things" (1983:123).

For the Shilluk, this incestuous performance encompasses an exercise in antisocial behavior and a turning inward of physical and social capacities by the major figure as society's attention is fixated on the literal center of their land. This suggests that the king of the Shilluk is more than a mediator between all the social domains which converge at the capital at installation. He is also conceived of as a source of power to destroy and create the rules which govern the other members of society. Finally, it should be noted that in order to insure the most complete transformation possible of the chosen individual, the electors are led to nominate from among those available the one with the most enviable social and personal record up to this point in his existence. This is, of course, a judicious political choice, since he will reign over them in a secular role. However, the selection also allows for the crucial element of personal transformation required by the process of creating a ruler who is also a divinity.

The interpretations suggested by the preceding analysis are partly constrained by some of the unique features of Shilluk culture. However, the connection between incest and power have widespread applicability across time and space. Any number of kingships in Africa and other parts of the traditional world have made this very equation. Indeed, some of our own myths, which may be regarded with respect to their message to the rituals of more traditional peoples, make a related point about incest and the means to power. The well-known tales of Oedipus Rex, King Arthur, and the royal Shakespearean tragedies forcefully inform us that mythical kingship is associated with the incestuous deed. Incest and power are inextricably linked in our minds with ascending to the existing political heights, as in the case of Oedipus, or in creating a new order out of chaos, as in the tale of Arthur.

The basic position adopted here is that incest is a product of both human imagination and capability. From this it follows that a main concern of the deed is with the transmission of profound cultural messages about what it means to be human. This points to a more complex and subtle set of ideas, not to be resolved by specific reference to the transmission of genes. This approach may have some value when considering the prohibition or avoidance of incest, but, as the evidence suggests, sociobiology lacks relevance when the violation calls for commentary. To return to the most popular example, it is Cleopatra as a product of the human political imagination, rather than biological issue, that demands attention. The standard sociological argument regarding an incestuous marriage as the only proper marital alliance for royalty also lacks interpretive substance.

Both the sociobiological and sociological explanations for incest turn their prevailing theories for the prohibition on end, as they view royal incest as an explicable, if not acceptable, genetic or social strategy. In some sense, these views are understandable, since the world of incestuous kings is one which is intentionally meant to invert the normal experience of the masses. However, when inversions of the moral order are culturally constructed for pantomime by a society's most significant characters or during moments of crisis, then scientific explanations for concrete activity fall short of the mark. There is no denying that if the presumed outcome of royal incest in the form of sex and reproduction were to follow, then sociobiology and sociology would offer some reasonable explanations for this problem, which has been on hand for some time now. However, the evidence for the past and present on these societies suggests that, in some cases, sex and reproduction are either difficult or impossible to document, or otherwise best presumed to be absent, as the principal actors engage in symbolic cultural performances having little to do with the mechanics of genetics or marital alliance.

To return to the primary example, it should be clear that the candidate for the Shilluk office and the ritual experts are attempting to construct a king with reference to the notion of incest. The understanding of a cultural system is called for, in contrast to scientific or social scientific explanations of a soluble problem. Understanding the essence of a compelling issue may not be as satisfactory to some as a crisp scientific explanation, but it is far superior to pseudoscience. Royal incest has attracted too much of the latter by incorporating folk concepts, popular imagery, ungrounded assumptions, and dubious evidence within an intellectual framework which has all the external marks of scientific procedure. This has resulted, not surprisingly, in a failure to offer a satisfactory explanation, but it also obscures, if not prevents, a reasonable grasp of the issue. What has been proposed instead admittedly fails to provide an explanation for royal incest in the sense of identifying the immediate cause and effect of the behavior. However, the argument offers some insight into what must be considered in confronting incest in one of its most imaginative human forms.

CHAPTER 9

The Power
of Incest (II)

. . . power is tolerable only on condition that it mask an
essential part of itself. Its success is proportional to its
ability to hide its own mechanisms.   FOUCAULT, 1980

WHETHER OR NOT the analysis of the meaning of incest offered in
the preceding chapter has any value for the incidence of the deed
in societies where it is unacceptable deserves consideration. Incest in
a forbidden moral context may initially call for other interpretations,
since the act is self-indulged, rather than dictated. Yet, the existing
sociobiological or sociological explanations for such human behavior
continue to offer little insight into these instances of violation. Marital or reproductive strategies have little relevance to the deed in societies such as our own, where illicit sex among family members is
the only issue. Incest in these situations may be sex for its own sake
or, alternately, it may mark other, less obvious, idiosyncratic com-
pulsions and personal statements. The latter demand attention in
light of the intimate relationship between incest and the quest for
and the demonstration of power in other cultural settings.

Our own brand of incest has been the intellectual domain of sociologists interested in deviance and psychologists with their curiosity for the human personality and its defects. As a result, there is a
broad literature on the topic, but many basic questions still remain.
For an example, the incidence of incest in our society, otherwise so
well documented in terms of personal behavior, remains undeter-
mined. This gap is due in part to the secretive nature of incestuous
behavior and the social embarrassment which surrounds involve-

ment, even for the victim. This lack of data is also due to a failure by social scientists to consider incest on both practical and theoretical levels. This condition prevails largely because of the influence of Freud and classical psychoanalysis, which relegated incest to the fantasy world of ego, rather than recognizing it as an actual sexual experience and tribulation of another person. This realization of incest for the trauma it may be for a victim has recently provoked many to raise a passionate alarm against traditional approaches to the problem.[1]

Despite this new concern for a more concrete view of human sexual behavior, other salient aspects of the problem still remain considerably blurred as the result of placing incest into the broad category of sexual abuse. At the level of emotions and personal trauma, these may be similar, but from the concern of this study incest takes on a special meaning and has to be examined apart from other deviant sexual behavior. As a consequence of the prevailing broad view of a now recognized social problem, it is difficult to determine the extent of coital incest. This is a significant concern, for although sexual behavior may legitimately be viewed as a physical and psychological process running along a continuum, the act of intercourse conveys with it the possibility of a more complete form of domination. This is particularly the case with an instigator and an unwilling partner. Sex in this context, as is now recognized, is primarily a display of power, calling for a particular form of interpretation.

There is also as noted earlier the enigma of determining the incidence and meaning of the potential heterosexual constellations in a typical nuclear family. Certain incestuous arrangements are assumed, with little supportive statistical evidence, to be more prevalent. More important, the different dyadic possibilities appear to evoke varying responses, since they impact in different ways on encompassing values and social categories by which humans interpret their interpersonal universe. Apparently responding in part to this framework, it is most often assumed that father-daughter incest is most prevalent in our society. As mentioned, this is the variation which most comes to the public attention. In addition, this arrangement also conforms to generalized notions about the relationship between the sexes in our society, which many would argue suffers from excessive masculine dominance. This view of sex accords well with the influential primal-horde image of the origin of the incest prohibition referred to earlier, which implies the voluntary or forceful relinquishing of male sexual rights over related females. However, in light of this pervasive view of the sexual authority of males, and possibly because of it, father-daughter incest conjures up the most obvious form of illegitimate power.

In such instances, one recourse for the family is to countenance such behavior, adding to the incidence of unreported cases of incest. Alternately, it is necessary in this instance to refer the matter to public agencies, which adds to the list of father-daughter cases. Moreover, when an incident becomes apparent, it is viewed with regret but nonetheless interpreted with some degree of community resignation, since the arrangement conforms to our expectations about the nature of males and authority in our society. Sexual norms may be violated, but those pertaining to the exercise of power are not contradicted. Thus father-daughter incest may be illicit, but also socially explicable. This situation has led some to suggest that a patriarchal family structure makes incest in some form an inevitable feature of the feminine social experience (Herman 1981).

The other possible incestuous alternatives, involving mother and son or sister and brother, evoke quite different reactions. The latter, depending on the broad range of potential sexual activity, is assumed by many others to be the most prevalent form of such behavior. However, it rarely comes to light, and then primarily by self-confession. Indeed, popular literature and imagination may even portray this peculiar relationship as a compelling, though doomed, romantic affair, worthy of a certain degree of curiosity and admiration. It is interesting that, in comparison to the father-daughter arrangement, it is often assumed that love may be a factor in drawing siblings together. This equation of incestuous sex and love likely derives from the presumed social equality of the pair, and thus the absence of outright domination by the male. This of course does not deny that in some instances force may be involved, but it is nonetheless clear that, for a variety of reasons, our society reserves a special emotive reaction to brother-sister incest which fails to involve public insult or horror.

The final possibility, which is unanimously assumed to be the most rare form of incest, conveys with it a double assault on expectations and sensibilities. As mentioned, those societies which have no apparent experience of incest and no stated prohibition react to the mention of mother-son sexual relations with incredulity. To many, this is an unimaginable relationship, while in our own society, where it has been detected in practice, the reaction is perplexity. Even the limited psychological literature on this subject portrays those implicated as severely disturbed, in comparison to those involved in the other forms.[2] Indeed, there is a general presumption that siblings, and even fathers and daughters, who enter into an incestuous relationship are relatively normal individuals, were it not for this abrogation of a sexual norm. The consequences of the affair, especially if made public, may have damaging psychological effects, particularly for the female in a father-daughter arrangement. However, it is more readily assumed by professional and lay opinion that a mother and son who engage in such behavior are already psychologically maladjusted individuals. Their illness or psychological abnormality results in incest, rather than the other way around.

There are obviously many reasons for this disparity in the incidence of incestuous relationships and variation in public emotive response. One pair of commentators (Frances and Frances 1976) argue that in Western society the healthy psychological development of the male entails the rejection of the early intense emotional and physical bond between mother and son. In the process, the father becomes the attractive role model in the growth of a son's normal masculine identity and adult personality. Assuming concomitant heterosexual identity on his part, this process poses no potential for interfamilial sexual behavior between parent and offspring. The existence of this close emotional and physical arrangement between mother and son in the formative years would preclude, according to sociobiologists, the formation of a similar qualitative relationship at a later point in the child's life with sexual maturity. This view of personality development also rests comfortably with Westermarck's notion of the consequences of early familiarity on later sexual attraction. For a variety of reasons, then, the mother becomes an avoided sexual object for the male offspring, and a subsequent attraction to her would indicate a failure of normal psychosocial and biological reactions. He would indeed have experienced abnormal development if he perceived of his mother as a sexual object as a young adolescent. For the mother, not all of these factors are involved, since the adult personality has already been formed, but the preclusion of bonds and avoidance response can be assumed to be relevant considerations, in conjunction with abiding ethical standards and responsibilities.

Considering the similar psychological process from the female perspective has a different outcome. According to this same view of normal personality development, the daughter must also experience this maturing "separation and individuation" from the mother. However, the resulting familial sociodynamics are quite different. The father also becomes the attractive role model and object of feminine affection. Assuming a concurrent heterosexual development on her part, the father then becomes a love object. The potential close physical and emotional relationship between father and daughter emerges with, or closer to, sexual maturity. In effect, the stage is set for incest with the development of the normal female personality. This interpretation of psychological maturity suggests that at least one of the roots of father-daughter incest lies within the groundwork of the emergence of a feminine personality in our society, given expression by the image of the seductive daughter. Even feminist social scientists (see Herman 1981) who have lately taken up the cause for a fresh interpretation of incest and its aftermath admit to this possibility. They note, however, that it is the moral responsibility of the adult to avoid taking advantage of such an inclination. This draws attention to the fact that the major barrier to father-daughter incest, in contrast to the mother-son variety, is an ethical standard undermined at least in part by the psychosocial dynamics of the family. If linked up with ideas of male dominance, it is not surprising that, in this atmosphere, father-daughter incest emerges as the common form of the violation of the taboo, which fails to confound public opinion.

The issue of the varying public response to the deed is also important to consider in greater detail from a sociological perspective. Sex between father and daughter implies a violation of a moral category, but many more assumptions are shaken when mother and son are presumed to engage in similar behavior. In this instance, notions of the proper authority structure in the domestic and public realms are assaulted. Mother-son incest makes it difficult to determine the aggressor and/or victim by confusing the notions of dominance and the expected categories of order, perception, and interpretation. Society, in the sense of ordered relationships and categories, is confounded with mother-son sexuality. Father-daughter incest is an expression of perverted order, while the opposite suggests the absence of order. Mother-son incest is an expression of the breakdown of all rules, and thus chaos. As such, it is unimaginable in some societies, while in others it is an indication of madness—a personal chaos.

Thus, in contrast to other forms of incest, the father-daughter variety implies that there is some order and shared meanings. This in turn suggests that the deed may be interpreted in part as a form of communication. The fact that the arrangement is socially unacceptable does not detract from the possibility of concurrent social discourse. As noted in other contexts, antisocial activity may draw attention to the nature of society's stated and unstated premises. This public understanding of the deed and its meaning in our social system deserves explication. Father-daughter incest is also the variation which has earned the most attention in the academic literature, so that the existence of the data on this type of domestic incest permits some insight into a form of antisocial communication.

According to the psychologists and therapists, the world and personality of the incestuous father and family is not particularly bizarre.[3] In many, if not most, instances, incestuous fathers are otherwise well adjusted (Maisch 1972 and Raphling 1967). The same condition holds, in many respects, for the other members and for the family. As revealed earlier, in the consideration of the recorded evidence on instances of incest, contrary to the assumptions of many, the family does not demonstrate undue role confusion, nor does it disintegrate under the presumed conflict and strain. Indeed, the opposite may be the case, as roles become interchangeable or are reassigned to different members, as the family insulates itself against prevailing moral standards and influences. What is apparent for these families, however, is the uncommon exercise of parental authority with the emergence of the father as the sole arbiter of morality and a corresponding withdrawal of the mother from a position of influence.[4] The mother, daughter, and other members of the household become passive bystanders and victims of an overbearing male, who often maintains overly rigid standards of proper social behavior in other areas. In effect, the father is often characterized as a domestic tyrant in maintaining some common norms, while contravening this most profound sexual standard. This behavior, including the incest itself, has the effect of isolating the family members from external social relationships, and as a result they become more rigidly dependent and constrained by the father's activities.

This display of power on the male's part may also be interpreted from a psychological viewpoint as juvenile and a reflection of an uncertain masculine identity, but this does not negate the social consequences of such behavior.[5] The idea of unlimited control over the domestic universe is explicitly stated, whatever its psychological origins. This characterization of the social atmosphere of the incestuous household is one of the most agreed-upon conclusions of the entire field of study. Emerging from this social context is the figure of an unrestrained potentate who exercises and validates his claim to authority in part by unrestrained sexuality. The fact that this behavioral statement flies in the face of acceptable standards is no matter. This abrogation of common morality provides the deed with profound social meaning. For the incestuous father in our society, the domestic universe replaces the external one as the relevant framework of experience. From this perspective, incest implies a sad and futile attempt to reconstruct a personal universe, which is decaying with the father's own physical decline and the maturity of its female members who, in the normal course of events, would establish their own domestic arrangements. As the initial social unit he created at marriage begins to disintegrate, the prime mover attempts to forestall the inevitable by an attempt at reproduction, which would revitalize his personal society.

The surrender of the female members of the family to others is an act of sociability and the admission of personal decline, which the incestuous father is unwilling to engage in. As Dubreuil (1962) argues, the incestuous male interprets society not as a benefit, but as a danger to his authority. As such, he not only limits his own participation in it, which is a typical feature of incestuous male personalities, but he also attempts to achieve the same restrictions on other family members. In the process, states Dubreuil, the incestuous father constructs his family on the model of a kingdom, where his own authority, rather than society's rulings, reigns supreme. There is no denying Lévi-Strauss's (1969) assertion that the exchange of women is an eminently social act which is negated by father-daughter incest. However, in light of what we now know about the mating patterns of other species, it becomes arguable, if not apparent, that the failure to exchange is the point where culture makes its negative appearance in human affairs. This human restriction on sociability is implied, whether the behavior is institutionalized and public as an aspect of legitimate authority or carried out in private as an expression of an illegitimate exercise.

This interpretation of the illicit deed and the regal imagery offered by Dubueil may be too imaginative, but it supports the contention that some wider meaning should be elicited, even when contending with uncondoned incest. The image of each man as a king in his own castle is tempting, but not totally satisfactory. However, there is no denying the thematic power element coloring incest, even in our social system, which is reminiscent of the royal instance. In both contexts, the deed exalts the individual over society. The intent of incest in other aspects may vary from society to society, but there is no escape from the common ideological link between sex and power, especially when the deed is antisocial in nature or reserved for the political elite. As others have noted in so many different social contexts, much apparent sexual behavior, in humans as well as for other primates, is in reality pseudosexual in nature, having little to do with reproduction, or even physical pleasure. Sexual behavior may be simultaneously and even primarily concerned with a display of personal aggression and domination, which are closely linked physiological and emotional states for humans and related species. As is now recognized, sex is often used as a means of establishing dominance, or an indication of existing superiority (Storr 1972). The sexual act, therefore, becomes doubly significant in these regards, if it is also antisocial and forbidden.

To some, it may seem a dubious procedure to attempt to draw parallels between institutionalized royal incest from archaic times and exotic places and unsanctioned sexual behavior in our era and society. There are many easily appreciated differences between the two social contexts. To choose one example, royal incest is enjoined by a particular people for the sake of how they conceive of their society, which requires in some profound sense that their political elite necessarily symbolize an incestuous relationship. The existence of the group is assumed to depend on the deed, and it is engaged in for the sake of society. As such, it is preeminently a social act.

The violation of the prohibition in our social system takes on an entirely different cultural interpretation. Domestic incest is viewed as personally irresponsible and a prime example of antisocial behavior, engaged in for the sake of individual gratification at the expense of the wider group. Another, and less apparent, difference between the two forms is the fact that royal incest is best understood in most instances as a symbolic performance, while incest in our society entails actual sexual behavior and, sometimes, reproduction. This second distinction has been misunderstood because of the failure to consider the cultural context and symbolic meaning of royal incestuous marriages. These examples cannot be equated with incestuous sex in societies where it is a factual violation of a sexual norm.

On the other hand, the two instances hint at some related meanings and contexts, the most obvious being, as suggested, the relationship between a forbidden sexual act and the exercise of power. At times, these may be inseparable notions, as one bespeaks the other, whether for heads of state or household. In the one instance, it may be deemed necessary in order to revitalize society, while in the other it serves as an indication of its decay. Yet in both contexts the incestuous idea or deed has profound implications for the definition of the exercise of power and the ability of the body and the individual to create new social forms. In neither case are the participants necessarily aware of this cultural intent or message. For kings, the incestuous relationship is entered into to act out a tradition which stretches back to the first human beings, or even beyond to the gods. This may not be a sufficient explanation for those who seek answers, but tradition is sufficient reason for those engaged as actors or members of society. In our more familiar context, it is the abrogation of tradition which gives the incestuous deed meaning, and this is also readily understood by the members of society.

Finally, it is worth restating that this consideration of the two incestuous styles has not been prompted by the quest for an ultimate explanation for the deed. Focusing on the potentially shared cultural meaning of incest in the varying contexts has little to offer directly in terms of origins and functions of the prohibitions, which are the more typical concerns of those interested in the problem. What has been sought instead is some understanding and deeper appreciation of incest as an element of culture. This approach stands in contrast to assigning incest to the category of historical oddity or psychosocial deviance. Such an exercise in classification generates an illusion of comprehension by the satisfying process of ordering cultural phenomena. Yet it is also equally reasonable to pause for a moment to consider in some detail what is being classified, since incest is one of our most profound and complex deeds.

CHAPTER 10

The Implications
of Incest

But we are not here concerned with hopes or fears, only
with the truth as far as reason allows us to discover it.

DARWIN, 1871

THE CONCLUDING REMARKS, whether to a mystery novel or academic
treatise, should be a tedious affair for both reader and writer alike.
According to protocol, the saving graces, assuming they have already visited such an occasion, should have departed. At this point
in the story line there should be no new characters, no startling dis-
coveries, and no surprises. The enigma should have already been resolved, rendering the conclusion a mandated exercise in redundancy
by appending another introduction to the end of a book. However,
this moment of reflection may also be profitable.

The course of this particular plot has moved from a consideration
of the genetic effects of inbreeding among the Amish of Lancaster,
Pennsylvania, to the making and meaning of divine kingship among
the Shilluk in the heart of the Sudan. Along the way, information
has been gleaned from a variety of academic disciplines often at
odds with each other as they view human nature and debate the
most profitable way to interpret this profound, though hazy, concept. In the process, some hoary general assumptions, which have
recognized no academic boundary, have been summarily dismissed
as unsubstantiated, while more novel suggestions of scholarly contention have been accepted as valuable insights resolving a long-
standing problem. Finally, the discussion has turned on incest rather
than around its opposite, leading to an equally antithetical conclusion

about the origin, function, and meaning of both the prohibition and commission of the deed. It is surprising, even to one familiar with the procedure, to recognize how the intentional inversion of a situation can eventually, if not inevitably, lead to contrary conclusions. There is inordinate value even in this simple intellectual exercise. The ideas and data which have guided this study are far from original in their parts. However, as befits the manner in which the question was posed, they have been ordered in a particular fashion to produce an unfamiliar result. As a consequence of this contextual alienation, there is ample opportunity for misinterpretation, potentially forestalled by summary and restatement.

The reactions of anthropological colleagues have already made it apparent[1] that some may interpret this argument about the cultural origin and significance of incest as merely a restatement of Lévi-Strauss's (1969:25) suggestion that the incest prohibition is not only cultural, but also the original cultural act. This common translation of the word "incest" into "incest prohibition" is a peculiar and interesting mental process which has been an explicit concern of this investigation. However, this prevailing unwitting inversion has served to mystify discussions of both phenomena, and indicates a failure of social science to confront incest as a distinct problem, deserving a rationale for its existence among humans. Therefore, it appears worthwhile to restate two basic conclusions which are, in fact, direct contradictions of Lévi-Strauss's formidable formulations, which have both stemmed from and subsequently reinforced traditional thinking.

First, it is argued here that the human pattern of outbreeding and the related practice of exogamy derive from an original innate avoidance of inbreeding, by a mechanism yet to be fully understood. Incest prohibitions which, as should now be appreciated, are not universal are cultural in origin. This varying outcome is due in part to social arrangements which can obviate or overcome this innate avoidance syndrome. This suggestion is far from original and not fully substantiated by conclusive evidence. However, it is revitalized by circumstantial data from other cultures, while other and apparently more popular assumptions on the origin of the incest prohibition have no resort to evidence of any sort. Indeed, much of the information on uncondoned incest, which goes unconsidered as irrelevant, renders most of the origin or functional arguments as little more than moral admonishments, and thus unacceptable as explanations for the prohibitions. Second, following from this interpretation of incest as an avoidance reaction, it has been advanced that the occurrence of incest is cultural in origin, rather than an expression of our animal nature or primal heritage. As with the prohibition, incest is also a human variable, beyond the ken and experience of some peoples, while institutionalized for others as a condoned and significant cultural act. Finally, it is engaged in, in other societies, as an unacceptable social act. The presumption of the human basis of incest compelled a search for the cultural meaning implied by the deed in its various social contexts. Although not offered as an explanation, or total comprehension of its meaning, it has been suggested that incest is an expression of potency, linked up with an indigenous notion of power.

This view of incest as a cultural product is a less familiar notion, and recognizably carries with it an uncomplimentary vision of human inventiveness. However, the alien nature and negative overtones of this idea must be judged as irrelevant considerations in seeking an explanation for the very existence and meaning of incest in human affairs. Moreover, despite these unenviable subjective interpretations, this conclusion does no injustice to the basic and shared contentions of science and social science about the significant capacity for culture as the distinguishing mark of our kind. Every student of human nature, past and present, agrees on this crucial distinction, which is not debated here. However, it must also be entertained, if not readily admitted, that the gift of culture carries with it no guarantee of moral superiority over other species. To commit incest and simultaneously condemn the deed are unique contradictory cultural abilities of the earth's most complex creature as it initially defines and then explores its moral boundaries.

Social scientists have long advocated an argument which elevates culture as the highest achievement of our kind, and have concentrated on and defended this position in the interpretation of human behavior. This belief needs no summarization. However, sociobiologists have also admitted as much, and in addition have been instrumental in redefining this achievement by refining our conception of culture. As Letourneau (1911:30), an early exponent of this view, suggested, humans are given to "caprice" in the conduct of their affairs. Lorenz (1971:225), a lifelong student of other species and careful interpreter of our own, updates this vision by proposing the recognition of "behavioral versatility" and "curiosity" in the sense of having both the ability and interest in experiencing what is possible as the preconditions of humanity. For Peter Wilson (1980: 14), it is "the brain as mind" which makes for what he optimistically refers to as "The Promising Primate."

In the course of the evolution of sexual behavior, this capacity has resulted in hypersexuality, which allows sex for its own sake or as a medium for conveying other messages about social relations. For humans, sexual activity and reproduction have become potentially distinct functions.[2] As a consequence of these varied abilities, incest can be expressed in the different forms considered here. However, these forms have little to do with an explicit attempt at reproduction. These human resorts to the imaginable are extensions of the mind, not organism. The failure of both scientists and social scientists to combine their respective insights about human nature has resulted in the inability to construe incest for what it is—a human monopoly. In contradiction to prevailing assumptions of both camps, culture does not deter a general or rare recourse to incest (Shepher 1983:179); it encourages or designs the appearance of the deed.

Arriving at this unsavory conclusion has involved coming to terms with the messages of traditional, though always embattled, social science and sociobiology. This confrontation is in part intellectual, since they each conjure up different visions of humanity in the form of constructing a boundary between man and beast. The conflict is also partially an academic matter which entails jurisdictional disputes, competing claims for institutional support and public attention. These features of the clash of forces account for the often bitter climate of the debate, as the morals, manners, and political philosophies of the disputants involved are sometimes called into consideration.

The continued vulnerability of social science has been due in part to its inability to provide a satisfactory solution to the question of the origin of the incest prohibition, which it has itself posed as one of the basic issues demanding resolution before advancing onto other problems. Successive generations of social scientists have invariably adopted a new explanatory model of human nature with reference to the prohibition of incest. Evolutionary theory, psychoanalysis, structural-functionalism, and structuralism have all implicitly assumed that this restriction on human sexuality is cultural in origin, while explicitly disagreeing on almost all else. In contrast to the paradigms of the exact sciences, which begin to crumble when new, unanswerable questions arise which cannot be elegantly resolved, the explanatory models of the social sciences begin immediately to disintegrate with the consideration of the same basic problems which caused the rejection of the previous model of human nature. The question of the origin and function of the incest rules are cases in point. One can only assume that it is the fascinating nature of the profound questions raised, rather than the record of accomplishments, which has attracted new adherents to the enterprise in each generation. Huxley was no doubt partially correct in his estimation when he defined the new discipline of anthropology as "a religion of man" (1863:261). Yet it is a peculiar religion which fails to provide an acceptable origin myth for the faithful. This failure in orthodoxy only invites continual disputation and schisms in every successive era.

In our time this typical unsettled intellectual atmosphere has spawned the new discipline of sociobiology, which avows to succeed where others have failed, by the wedding of social science to natural science. Not surprisingly, it stakes its claim to respectability by offering a solution to the questions of the origin and function of the incest rules. There is no denying that adherents to the new message have added immeasurably to an understanding of these problems and, for the moment at least, have their opponents in retreat and a state of dismay. This is to be expected, since any science has a major cultural advantage over traditional anthropology, which now bears the brunt of the assault. The sociobiologists' secret weapon, in many senses of the phrase, is the ability to convert their arguments into mathematical formulae, while their anthropological opponents continue to rely on mere words and the occasional kinship diagram. Thus one encounters in the new liturgy of sociobiology an essay (Kurland 1979) on human breeding which begins with the rendition of a line from Shakespeare and ends with

$$p > \frac{2}{1+e} - \left[\frac{4}{(1+e)^2} - 1\right]\frac{1}{2}$$

The advantages of being able to couch a problem and its resolution in such a fashion are inestimable in a culture which places a premium on the symbols of science and defines in part the value of an intellectual inquiry in terms of its inexplicability.

The weakness of sociobiology is the intellectual appetite of its founders, which is succeeded only by the rapaciousness of new converts to the fold from other disciplines who have heard the call. To many anthropologists it may seem that this new synthesis is intent on devouring their subject matter whole. They thus react against the onslaught with the expected display of defensive outrage. Yet this novel discipline asserts itself with the same lack of modesty which characterized anthropology only a century ago, when it claimed to explicate cultural difference by recourse to the universal laws of social evolution. The accumulation of data, and thus a finer appreciation of the problems at hand, often as not temper initial bursts of enthusiasm. This was the case for anthropology, and the same sobering experience is undoubtedly in store for sociobiology as it eventually comes to realize that the expression of unevidenced folk concepts and popular assumptions about incest in mathematical symbols and a scientific vocabulary carries with it little real intellectual advantage.[3] Whatever the value of sociobiology in clarifying the nature of incest rules as a reflection of an avoidance syndrome common to a number of species, its attempts at advancing this framework as an explanation for human kinship and marital behavior on similar grounds have been far from satisfactory. This naiveté is no more apparent than with the consideration of royal incest, where adherents continue to assume, as did nineteenth-century theorists, that sex and marriage are synonymous. Victorian social commentators may be excused for conveying such a moral message in their arguments, but those in our time who claim to have their theories grounded in the facts of life have learned little about human social and cultural imagination. There are few limits on the human ability and interest to confound biological and social rules. Those interested in such topics have little to fear from others who enter the fray armed with the symbols of science.

Finally, there are the implications of the nature of the conclusion about the culture of incest, which has been arrived at by an unfamiliar arrangement of the information. It can only be suggested, as with Darwin, who is so often called upon to legitimize these inquiries, that, hopes and fears for humanity notwithstanding, only the truth of the matter should guide an inquiry into our nature. The failure to pay heed to this advice has been an inherent feature of the history of this intellectual complex. At times it has generated an inexplicable inability to construe an objective vision of this situation, and then reasonable arguments, even by some of the true giants of social science.

If it be correct that, in a convoluted way, nature is responsible for a rule prohibiting incest and, in an equally complex fashion, culture is responsible for its appearance in human affairs, then this may require some revision of thought. The familiar idea that culture is superior to nature may be comfortable to contemplate by the one and only cultured species, but this vision has never been demonstrated to have an objective basis. Irony may be another perplexing monopoly of our kind.

Notes

Chapter 1

1. The only major figure of nineteenth-century social science to have avoided the issue was Max Weber.
2. See, for example, Shepher's *Incest: A Biosocial View*; Slater's "Ecological Factors in the Origin of Incest"; Livingstone's "Genetics, Ecology, and the Origins of Incest and Exogamy"; and Mead's encyclopedia item "Incest." For a concrete example, consider Livingstone's statement, ". . . the origins of incest and exogamy must be sought elsewhere" (1969:46). It is clear from the context of the discussion that the author was referring to and meant to say the incest taboo rather than "incest."
3. This genre has become voluminous in a short period. See Armstrong (1979), Bass and Thorton (1983), and Brady (1979).
4. For a different interpretation, see Hertier (1982).
5. These situations would be violations of exogamous prescriptions, that is, rules pertaining to marriage rather than sexual delicts. However, the latter may also be involved. The distinctions between sexual and marriage regulations, and the question of whether or not sex and reproduction were also involved, are taken up later.
6. See Marett's elegant statement, ". . . the incest taboo takes no interest in marriage whatsoever" (1932:60).
7. For a sophisticated treatment of the relationship between sexual and marriage prohibitions among the Bara of Madagascar, see Huntington (1978).
8. This has already been admirably done by Robin Fox, most notably in *Kinship and Marriage*. For another example, see Frank Vivelo's *Cultural Anthropology Handbook*. Both make immediate sense of what has gone before, while Fox's original contributions have added greatly to an appreciation of the problem and its resolution.
9. This theme has been explored by Luc de Heusch in a series of publications (de Heusch 1958 and 1962). Cohen (1977) has also responded to some of de Heusch's interpretations.

Chapter 2

1. This was determined by the admission of both parties and blood tests on the males to determine if they could not have been the biological fathers. In all cases, their blood type matched the children's, and therefore they could not be excluded as a potential parent.

2. The twelve brother-sister pairs were described as being from the middle class, and the father-daughter pairs, from the lower class. The authors also state that the incestuous mothers placed in the "dull" category as far as their IQs were concerned. This factor may not be an explanation for engaging in incest, but may explain why they became pregnant. Interestingly enough, comparable data on the males' intelligence were unavailable, nor was there any indication as to whether or not coercion of the female was involved. Intimidation is a reasonable assumption for father-daughter instances, since the male is, by definition, an authority figure, but this may or may not be a factor with brothers and sisters.

3. The principal instance here involves a long-term study and a series of reports on cousin marriage in Japan (Neel 1958, Schull 1958 and 1972, and Schull and Neel 1972). A summary of the results and related studies can be found in Schull and Neel (1965).

4. In addition to Schull and Neel, cited above, these studies include Book (1957), Hammond and Jackson (1958), Slatis (1958), Sutter (1958), and Sutter and Tabah (1951).

5. This factor was also noted by Hussien (1971) in a study of the same phenomenon in Egypt.

6. For a good discussion of the issue, see Stern (1973:489–499).

Chapter 3

1. For an example of this approach and an assessment of explanations, see Aberle et al. (1963).

2. The quotations are from the 1950 edition of Bentham's *Theory of Legislation*, pp. 217–218.

3. For an extended discussion of prevailing attitudes toward the function of the incest prohibition in the eighteenth century, see Aldridge (1951).

4. As noted earlier, Morgan's schema was adopted, with some liberties, by Engels in 1884 when he proclaimed that marriage between parents and offspring was still permissible in some parts of the world (1942:31).

5. The initial information on such an anomaly derives from Malinowski's research on the Trobriand Islands off New Guinea, reported in *The Sexual Life of Savages*, pp. 201–202 and passim. This oddity has spurred an often acrimonious debate, primarily between Leach (1967) and Spiro (1968). Additional ethnographic support for Malinowski's original account of the Trobrianders is offered by Monberg's (1975) work on the Bellona of the Solomon Islands. The author states and accepts the native argument that they were formerly ignorant of the biological relationship between sex, which they considered a pleasant pastime, and reproduction.

6. In the context of this discussion, Fox mentions that there are actually some societies which allow for father-daughter sex, but prohibit marriage (1983:57). However, he offers no specific example or citation from a literary source for this interesting contention.

7. This is not meant to take issue with Gay's (1984) revisionist interpretation of Victorian sexuality. Whatever the true state of affairs, they could not compare to the images of sexuality in other cultures, portrayed by Victorian social theorists.

8. See Needham's (1976:xxix) more extensive comments on this subject in his Editor's Introduction to Starcke (1976). He also draws attention to Gay Weber's contention that this rejection of the primitive-promiscuity hypothesis in Wake's case was due to "a revulsion" against the idea of incest, since it diminished "human dignity" (Weber 1974:278). There is little evidence to support Weber's more subjective interpretation of the situation, nor, if so, would this necessarily be mutually exclusive of more rigorous evidential standards on Wake's part.

9. Needham's introduction to Hocart's *Kings and Councillors* also draws attention to the importance of holding a prominent academic position in having one's views accepted and subsequently remembered (1970:xc–xci). In contrast to Tylor and Frazer, at least, Wake and Starcke were not afforded the luxury of an academic sinecure.

On the issue of an intellectual foil, see Montagu's (1956) edition of, and comments on, an attenuated BBC debate in 1930 between Robert Briffault, a latter-day evolutionist, and Bronislaw Malinowski, a founder of the functionalist school, which eschewed conjectural history. Although they took a liking to each other on meeting, the radio exchanges became so acrimonious, Montagu reports, that the final one was abandoned by mutual agreement.

Up to that point Malinowski, who was Professor of Anthropology at the London School of Economics, was inclined to seek some sort of academic appointment for Briffault, who had none.

10. Ann Parsons (1970) has provided a more recent consideration of the varieties of cultural expressions of the Oedipal complex, based on her anthropological and psychoanalytic interpretations of unconscious familial sexuality in southern Italy.

11. See Blumenthal's (1981) article in *The New York Times* and Malcolm's (1983) essays in *The New Yorker*, prior to the publication of her book on the same subject and cast of characters (Malcolm 1984).

12. Interestingly enough, in his "wolf-man" case, Freud (1955) recognized the role incest played in this male patient's later psychopathology. The female involved in this borther-sister incident later committed suicide, so that the patient's guilt was obviously compounded by this factor.

13. This charge is levelled at contemporary psychotherapy by one of the main characters in the running feud on the significance and reasons for Freud's denial of incest (see Malcolm 1984).

14. See Krober's (1920 and 1939) earlier critical commentaries and Freeman's (1970) more contemporary estimation. The latter includes an evaluation of Freud's argument from the perspective of what is now known about the mating patterns of other animals, and how this bears on Freud's contentions about human behavior. In contrast, Fox (1967) has been more sympathetic to Freud's analysis on a variety of issues, including the varying interpretation on incest in the context of different descent systems raised by Goody's (1969) remarks on incest and adultery. For a recent overview of the anthropological response to Freud's *Totem and Taboo*, see Wallace (1983).

15. A similar "culturological" position was adopted at the same time by the American anthropologist Leslie White (1948), who traced the idea of the advantages of exogamy through Tylor to St. Augustine's *The City of God*. In a subsequent publication, White identified the prohibition of incest as the first "ethical act of history," which marked the beginning of human social evolution (1975:32).

Chapter 4

1. In all editions, Kroeber was rendered as "Kroeger," which Malinowski deemed almost "unpardonable" and only explicable in

terms of Freud's own dictum that no mistake is made without its motive.

2. Such an argument was not totally original, even with Malinowski, since the confusion idea he adopted was alluded to by Starcke some forty years earlier as ". . . quite enough to produce an aversion to such marriages" (1976:229).

3. This is a rather unusual form and place to encounter such information, since textbooks rarely interject new and controversial information, especially in such a vague style.

4. I am aware that this line of reasoning, which is now prevalent, sometimes even places partial responsibility for the affair on the daughter involved (see Bender and Blau 1937 and Raphling 1967), and thus implicitly diminishes the culpability of the father (see, for example, Henderson 1972 and Machotka 1967). This inclination, which holds the victim partially at fault for the crime, has been reasonably attacked by Herman (1981), who maintains that the father, as the dominant authority figure, has the onus to avoid or discourage familial sexuality, regardless of how initiated.

5. The conclusion that incest may not always have severe psychological effects on the female participants has been advanced by a number of psychologists. Their conclusions derive from a consideration of the differing effects related to the age of onset of the relationship and the degree of female compliance. See Maisch (1972), Sloane and Karpinski (1942), Schultz (1979), and Yorukoglu and Kemph (1966). Their argument, that this may be an outcome in some, though not even in a majority of cases, has been attacked by feminist authors.

Chapter 5

1. There was one immediate response, which argued in contradiction and without Wallis's novelty, that when humans did inbreed they would have recognized the biological advantages (Rose 1951).

2. Neither the text nor the bibliography makes reference to Wallis's precedence. Moreover, the article's obvious aim is to account for the origin of the prohibition, rather than, as the title suggests, "The Origin of Incest."

3. Initial reactions came from Moore (1960 and 1964). In these and subsequent discussions, Slater's name is almost invariably linked to this argument, while the originator goes unmentioned.

4. For recent evaluations of Westermarck, see Stroup (1982 and 1984).

5. He divided his time as Professor of Practical Philosophy at Helsingfors in his native Finland and Professor of Sociology at the University of London, but carried out his main teaching there, at the London School of Economics, because of its emphasis on the social sciences. He ended his academic career in Finland as rector of Abo Academy.

6. See Murdock's (1965:291) restatement of Frazer's objection.

7. In commenting on the impact of increased life expectancy on marriage, a former teacher remarked, with both humor and insight, that the divorce lawyer now replaces the undertaker in dissolving marriages which have exceeded the forbearance of those involved.

8. A summary of criticisms and the responses are contained in Westermarck's (1929:66–109) abbreviated version of his larger study. All references are to this summary restatement of Westermarck's argument.

9. Frazer was here quoting from *The Origin and Development of the Moral Ideas* (1971 [1906–08], Vol. II:364).

10. As a telling indication of the times, Westermarck (1929:98) mentions in his autobiography that his original book on marriage was so well received by the "Women's Movement" that he was chosen as vice-president of two feminist societies. He was somewhat embarrassed by this honor, since the attention derived from a concluding sentence, inserted by his editor, that the improvement of the status of women went together with the advance of civilization. Yet, improved women's rights and status were values Westermarck personally subscribed to, so he accepted the offices. Robin Fox, on the other hand, has yet to be singled out for such a distinction by contemporary feminists.

11. These include Wolf (1966, 1968, and 1970) and Wolf and Huang (1980).

12. This information was apparently derived from those directly involved or close confidants (see Wolf 1970:511).

13. M. Wolf (1968) has provided a more extensive discussion of this situation and the traditional position of women in Chinese society.

14. These include Harris (1971), Kirkpatrick (1972), Korbin (1981), Rosenblatt (1974), and Spiro (1982).

15. A preliminary report by McC. Pastner (1982) on a similar marriage form for a Pakistani community contradicts these results. However, she also notes that the age difference between the spouses, with the male an average of seven years older, precluded close childhood association, which is a crucial element of the

Westermarck hypothesis. Moreover, sexual segregation during childhood is also severe. These factors lead the author to suggest that the aversion effect may be eliminated or mitigated by intervening cultural variables.

16. Spiro argues that the earlier onset of puberty among the girls made boys of the same age unacceptable romantic partners. According to him, the males were "put off—even frightened—by the girls" (1982:153), and as a result the cosocialized peers were a physiologically mismatched group, which explained the lack of sexual attraction after puberty.

17. Kaffman (1977) proposed that puritanical attitudes of the time accounted for the lack of sexual behavior among the members of the same age cohort. He claims, without factual support, that the relaxed sexual standards of the 1970s resulted in affairs of this sort, but the data continue to indicate a lack of subsequent marriages.

18. Of the total, a few marriages were contracted between peers from the same kibbutz, but the cosocialization was not complete, as one of the partners had entered the group at a later age, or left for a number of years and then returned to it.

19. This is a complex issue, for if the Westermarck effect were operative, then these affairs might be interpreted by those involved as "incestuous" in some cognitive sense and thus kept a secret. However, this situation would also support the avoidance argument, since such behavior was deemed shameful. In any event, from what is known about the violation of the stated and active prohibition in other domestic arrangements, it is imaginable that some heterosexual activity takes place among peers in the kibbutz, but these are rare occurrences.

20. This possibility was touched on by Fox (1962:147) and others in a more general interpretation of Freud's worldview, but has gone unconsidered in the case of Westermarck, presumably since his ideas have had less impact on our view of human nature.

Chapter 6

1. Quoted in Thomas's (1983:127) fascinating study of the changing views of animals and nature in Western thought.

2. For some indication of the problems involved, see Kroeber and Kluckhohn (1952).

3. Bischof admits to inbreeding among three groups, which include (1) lower orders with high reproductive rates and ecologic conditions which preclude outbreeding, especially apparent with para

sites, such as mites and worms; (2) domesticated animals whose breeding patterns are influenced by humans; and (3) zoo animals whose social patterns are also artificially interfered with by human arrangements (1975:56).

4. Studies which substantiate this position include Alexander (1970), Goodall (1967), Kaufman (1965), Kummer (1968), Packer (1979), Pusey (1980), Sade (1968), Starin (1981), and Veit (1982). A contrast to this pattern was recorded by Missakian (1973), who reports in her study of rhesus monkeys that 5.4 percent of sexual activity involved mother-son pairs and another 12 percent involved siblings. In response, Bixler (1981:640) notes that this behavior took place in times of stress and did not result in pregnancy. Moreover, those involved were juvenile males who moved out of their natal group upon sexual maturity. This is also the normal pattern for these primates.

5. One observation of mother-son mating involved the male successfully overcoming the female rejections and establishing dominance (Sade 1968:31–32). No specific information is provided on sibling mating, though this would be precluded in the main by male transference to another group.

6. Less relevant information is available for the hamadryas baboons of Ethiopia, but Kummer (1968:71) does report that mature males are sexually indifferent to their offspring, who are appropriated by other males.

7. In a recent response to the suggestion that group transfer is a feature of natural selection concerned with reducing inbreeding, Moore and Ali (1984) have offered a cautionary note, suggesting that other social factors such as territoriality or intrasexual competition might be more important causative agents of this mobility.

8. See, for example, the sweeping conclusions of Lumsden and Wilson (1981 and 1983).

9. For a general discussion of this issue, see Lancaster (1984).

10. See also Bateson (1978), Hill (1974), and Segner (1968).

11. See Harris (1975), Kettel (1982), and Murdock (1965). They object most vehemently, as have others (Lévi-Strauss 1969), to the idea of "instinct." A resort to this vague concept is admittedly unacceptable and not used in conjunction with the present avoidance argument.

12. Smith and Kennedy (1960) have also noted the ecological and demographic constraints on cultural extensions of the prohibition

by the comparison of these rules on a number of culturally related islands in Micronesia.

13. Fox (1975) has been the staunchest opponent of this view in social anthropology, but even Fortes (1983), a more traditional student of human kinship, was able to find agreement with this conclusion about the significance of cultural rules as opposed to behavior and social organization, which often corresponds between human and nonhuman primates. This idea has even found its way into one introductory anthropology, a literary genre not known for the adoption of novel approaches. Reference is made to Swartz and Jordon's (1976:235–236) concept of "protomortality" as a characteristic of primate behavior in the context of their discussion of incest "inhibitions."

14. Again suggesting that there may be no new ideas, it must be noted that in his dialogue with Freud over the Oedipal complex, Malinowski wrote: "The temptation to incest, therefore, has been introduced by human nature. . . . It is therefore, in a sense, the original sin of man" (1927:252). Malinowski was not entirely explicit in his reasoning for arriving at this conclusion, but the statement was preceded by mention of his belief that inbreeding was rare among animals, and incest was only a moral issue for humans because of our capacity for culture. Malinowski did not develop the significance or implications of this idea, especially with regard to a definition of human nature, but it was a profound insight.

15. This would seem to imply for Fox (1962) that incest is also cultural, but the explicit nature of this conclusion was not made, since his concern was with an account for the prohibition, rather than incest.

Chapter 7

1. See Aberle et al. (1963), Harris (1975), and Vivelo (1978).
2. The inspiration for such an approach is Hamilton's (1963 and 1964) notion of "inclusive fitness," which is the content of an individual's genetic representation over time. Recent explorations of this and related concepts are to be found in Chagnon and Irons (1979).
3. An extensive consideration of this problem is the subject of a special issue of the *Journal of the Polynesian Society*, edited by

Schneider (1976). See in particular the contributions by Fischer et al., Hooper, and Labby. Also see Fischer (1950) and Beidelman (1971).

4. For indications of the difficulties involved in explicating traditional terminological and marriage systems among peoples erroneously presumed to have engaged in incestuous marriages, see the contemporary ethnographic analyses of this complex issue by Faron (1956) and Needham (1962).

5. As noted earlier, a further exception has been noted for the Egyptian middle class by Middleton (1962) and Hopkins (1980), with reasonable historical documentation.

6. Since sociobiologists have argued that outbreeding is a natural tendency, incest presents a complexity for the paradigm, and as such has received little attention, except the observation that it is rare (see Shepher 1983). The argument summarized here follows Van Den Berghe and Mesher (1980). See also Van Den Berghe and Mesher (1981), Van Den Berghe and Barash (1977), and Sturtevant's (1981) reply.

7. It is interesting that Fox's (1962) discussion of this subject and his evidence, which sorts out the issues, tend to be ignored by those committed to either an attraction or an avoidance assumption. Neither side seems to be particularly interested in the facts, which do not offer wholehearted support for either contention.

8. This conclusion is admitted to by Van Den Berghe and Mesher (1980:313), who suggest that royal incest is not genetically determined. They aver that this consideration of sociobiological consequences needs to be recognized, rather than assuming that cultural adaptation is random and unconcerned with biological factors.

9. Cerney (1954) argues quite reasonably from his review of the preserved written record that in order to conclude with assurance if some sort of sibling marriage had taken place, it is necessary to determine the names of both the mother and father of the couple. In maintaining this strict standard of evidence, he was able to determine from 490 unions only three cases of half-sibling marriage and none of full brother and sister. For a latter period during the Roman occupation, Hopkins (1980:304) alludes to a far greater number, with reference to fifteen to twenty-one percent of all marriages being between some sort of siblings. This substantiates an earlier claim by Middleton (1962).

10. These include Cerney (1954), Hopkins (1980), Middleton (1962), and Ruffer (1921).

11. Bixler's evaluation of the literature on Peru, Hawaii, and Thailand, which are not as surely documented as Egypt for royal marriages, leads him also to conclude that these arrangements were not intended to produce an heir to the throne. There is even less documentation to assume that this outcome was ever the case.
12. Bixler is also a devotee of the Westermarck hypothesis. Thus he argues that the relative absence of a sexual and reproductive element in these arrangements has no negative bearing on the aversion syndrome. He also assumes, as does the sociobiological interpretation of royal incest, that living arrangements in a royal household would probably not generate an avoidance reaction.
13. Reference is made to the argument that the incest of divine royalty can be accounted for as a reflection on the behavior of gods. This is merely a restatement of the problem in different terms, rather than an explanation.
14. His relevant publications are listed in the bibliography.
15. This summary is taken from Krige and Krige (1943) and Krige (1975). For the closely related Swazi kingship, see Kuper (1947).
16. In her latest publication on the subject, Krige (1975:60) reports that most successors have been the offspring of a half-sibling union. The author's discussion of this fact, however, is neither very extensive nor capable of documentation, since the queen who does not marry may discreetly have sexual relations with other men.
17. Van Den Berghe and Mescher (1980), who offer the interpretative model, do not include the Lovedu in their list of incestuous kingdoms, but they do consider the Shilluk, which is a highly suspect example on ethnographic grounds. The case is discussed in detail in the following chapter.
18. See Leach (1969) and Leach and Aycock (1983).

Chapter 8

1. Preliminary archival and field research in the southern Sudan among the Shilluk was carried out by the author for three months in 1978. The project was supported by a postdoctoral research grant from the American Social Science Research Council and conducted under the aegis of the Institute for African and Asian Studies, University of Khartoum. Reports on these people, with specific reference to their kingship, are to be found in Arens (1979b, 1984, and 1986). Previous commentators include Evans-Pritchard (1948), Frost (1974), Hofmayr (1911 and 1925), Lien-

hardt (1954), Mercer (1971), Riad (1956), and Seligman and Seligman (1932).

2. This literature has been admirably collated and interpreted by Mercer (1971).

3. The Shilluk have been under intermittent external control and threat for over a century, beginning with the presence of representatives of the Ottoman empire in 1867 and ending with their incorporation into an independent nation-state, so that the traditional political authority of their king is difficult to reconstruct. In addition, the Shilluk have a polydynastic system governing inheritance of the office. As a result, there are always disgruntled pretenders to the throne in various parts of the country, with their own political support groups. The issue of the king's authority in the context of these historical facts and political complexities is addressed in Arens (1979b).

4. An excellent discussion of this particular case and other funerary rituals is provided by Huntington and Metcalf (1979).

5. See, for example, the ethnographic analyses and general overviews of Arens (1979b), Richards (1969), M. Wilson (1959), and Young (1966).

6. These rituals were not observed during the course of fieldwork. The commentary is made possible by a reanalysis of the accounts of Howell (1944, 1952a, 1952b, and 1953), Howell and Thompson (1946), and Munro (1918). All were European officers of the Sudan Political Service in the years prior to independence.

7. Van Den Berghe and Mesher consider the Shilluk as an instance having "Reliable evidence that actual coitus took place between close kin" (1980:305–306). Despite their exact mathematical expression of the genetic relationship, it is a dubious conclusion to assume that marriage, sex, or reproduction were involved.

8. See Shils's (1965) interpretation of Weber and Geertz's (1983) comments on Shils.

Chapter 9

1. See Herman (1981) and Rush (1980).

2. Studies of this topic are rare, but see, as an example, Henderson (1975). Raphling (1967:510) notes from a case study that a wife who "passively" accepted incest between her husband and daughter was "revolted" when her son made sexual advances toward her.

3. My concern here is with the potential social meaning of incest, which is a different matter from that of personal psychological

trauma and guilt for those who may be involved. This is another issue, and not denied.

4. A peculiar feature of the literature on father-daughter incest is the availability of almost as much information on the personality and function of the mother, who is now often seen as psychologically denying this relationship or lending tacit approval to it by failing to exercise proper moral judgment and authority (see Henderson 1972).

5. This is a common psychological interpretation. See Cormier et al. (1962) and Lustig et al. (1966).

Chapter 10

1. An abbreviated form of this argument has been presented in lecture form on various occasions.

2. For a detailed discussion of this topic, see Jensen (1973) and Rosenzweig (1973).

3. See Callan's (1984) discussion of the metaphors and imagery of sociobiology.

Bibliography

Aberle, David F., et al. 1963. The Incest Taboo and the Mating Patterns of Animals. *American Anthropologist* 65:253–264.

Adams, Morton, et al. 1967. Adoptive Risks of the Children of Incest. *Child Welfare* 46:137–142.

Adams, Morton, and James Neel. 1967. Children of Incest. *Pediatrics* 40:55–62.

Aldridge, A. O. 1951. The Meaning of Incest from Hutcheson to Gibbon. *Ethics* 61:309–313.

Alexander, B. K. 1970. Parental Behavior of Adult Male Japanese Monkeys. *Behavior* 36:270–285.

Arens, W. 1979a. *The Man-Eating Myth*. New York: Oxford University Press.

Arens, W. 1979b. The Divine Kingship of the Shilluk: A Contemporary Evaluation. *Ethnos* 3–4:167–181.

Arens, W. 1984. The Demise of Kings and the Meaning of Kingship. *Anthropos* 79:355–467.

Arens, W. 1986. The Power of Incest. In W. Arens and Ivan Karp (eds.), *The Creativity of Power*. Washington D.C.: Smithsonian Institution Press (in press).

Armstrong, Louise. 1979. *Kiss Daddy Goodnight*. New York: Pocket Books.

Bagley, Christopher. 1969. Incest Behavior and Incest Taboo. *Social Problems* 16:505–519.

Bass, Ellen, and Louise Thornton. 1983. *I Never Told Anyone*. New York: Harper and Row.

Bateson, Patrick. 1978. Sexual Imprinting and Optimal Outbreeding. *Nature* 273:659–660.

Beidelman, T. O. 1966. Swazi Royal Ritual. *Africa* 36:373–405.

Beidelman, T. O. 1971. Some Kaguru Notions about Incest and Other Sexual Prohibitions. In Rodney Needham (ed.), *Rethinking Kinship and Marriage*. London: Tavistock Publications.

Bender, L., and A. Blau. 1937. The Reactions of Children to Sexual Relations with Adults. *American Journal of Orthopsychiatry* 7:500–518.

Bentham, Jeremy, 1950. *Theory of Legislation*. London: Routledge and Kegan Paul.

Bischof, Norbert. 1975. Comparative Ethnology of Incest Avoidance. In Robin Fox (ed.). *Biosocial Anthropology*. London: Malaby Press.

Bixler, Ray H. 1981. Incest Avoidance as a Function of Environment and Heredity. *Current Anthropology* 22:639–654.

Bixler, Ray H. 1982a. Sibling Incest in the Royal Families of Egypt, Peru, and Hawaii. *The Journal of Sex Research* 18:264–281.

Bixler, Ray H. 1982b. Comment on the Incidence and Purpose of Royal Sibling Incest. *American Ethnologist* 9:580–582.

Blumenthal, Ralph. 1981. Scholars Seek the Hidden Freud in New Emerging Letters. *The New York Times*. Aug. 18, 1981:C1.

Böök, J. A. 1957. Genetical Investigations in a North Swedish Population. *American Journal of Human Genetics* 10:191–221.

Brady, Katherine. 1979. *Father's Days*. New York: Seaview Books.

Breuer, J., and S. Freud. 1955. Studies on Hysteria (1893–1895). In J. Strachey (ed.), *The Complete Works of Sigmund Freud*. Vol. II. London: Hogarth Press.

Briffault, Robert. 1927. *The Mothers*. New York: Macmillan.

Briffault, Robert, and Bronislaw Malinowski. 1956. *Marriage: Past and Present*. Boston: Porter Sargent.

Bruce, James. 1905. *Travels to Discover the Source of the Nile*. New York: Horizon Press.

Burnham, Jeffrey T. 1975. Incest Avoidance and Social Evolution. *Mankind* 10:93–98.

Burton, Roger. 1973. Folk Theory and the Incest Taboo. *Ethos* 1:504–506.

Busch, R. C., and J. Gundlach. 1977. Excess Access and Incest. *American Anthropologist* 79:912–914.

Callan, Hilary. 1984. The Imagery of Choice in Sociobiology. *Man* 19:404–420.

Carter, C. O. 1967. Risk to Offspring of Incest. *Lancet* 1:436.

Cavalli-Sforza, L. L., and W. F. Bodmer. 1971. *The Genetics of Human Populations*. San Francisco: Freeman.

Cerney, Jaroslav. 1954. Consanguineous Marriages in Pharaonic Egypt. *Journal of Egyptian Archaeology* 40:27–29.

Chagnon, Napoleon. 1981. Natural Selection and the Evolution of Human Kinship and Reproductive Systems. *Sociobiology* 6:23–45.

Chagnon, Napoleon, and William Irons (eds.). 1979. *Evolutionary*

Biology and Human Social Behavior. North Scituate, Mass.: Duxbury Press.

Cohen, Ronald. 1977. Oedipus Rex and Regina: The Queen Mother in Africa. *Africa* 47:14–30.

Cohen, Yehudi. 1964. *The Transition from Childhood to Adolescence*. Chicago: Aldine Publishing Company.

Cormier, Bruno, et al. 1962. Psychodynamics of Father-Daughter Incest. *Canadian Psychiatric Association Journal* 7:203–217.

Crawley, Ernest. 1960 (1902). *The Mystic Rose*. New York: Meridian Books.

Cross, Harold, and Victor McKusick. 1978. Amish Demography. In Victor McKusick (ed.), *Material Genetic Studies of the Amish*. Baltimore: Johns Hopkins University Press.

Darwin, Charles. 1981 (1871). *The Descent of Man and Selection in Relation to Sex*. Princeton: Princeton University Press.

Davis, Kingsley. 1965. *Human Society*. New York: Macmillan.

de Heusch, Luc. 1958. *Essais sur le symbolisme de l'inceste royal en Afrique*. Brussels: Université Libre de Bruxelles.

de Heusch, Luc. 1962. *Le pouvoir et le sacre*. Brussels: Annales du Centre d'Etude des Religions, Universite Libre de Bruxelles.

de Heusch, Luc. 1972. *Le roi ivre*. Paris: Gallimard.

de Heusch, Luc. 1975. What Shall We Do with the Drunken King? *Africa* 45:363–372.

de Heusch, Luc. 1981. *Why Marry Her?* Cambridge: Cambridge University Press.

de Heusch, Luc. 1982. *Rois nes d'un coeur de vache*. Paris: Gallimard.

Demarest, William. 1977. Incest Avoidance among Human and Non-Human Primates. In Suzanne Chevalier-Skolnikoff and Frank Poirier (eds.), *Primate Bio-Social Development*. New York: Garland Publishing Company.

Douglas-Hamilton, Iain, and Oria Douglas-Hamilton. 1975. *Among the Elephants*. New York: Viking Press.

Dubreuil, Guy. 1962. Les bases psycho-culturelles du tabou de l'inceste. *Canadian Psychiatric Association Journal* 7:218–234.

Durkheim, Emile. 1963 (1898). *Incest: The Nature and Origin of the Taboo*. New York: Lyle Stuart.

Eisenstadt, S. N. 1968. Editor's Introduction to Max Weber, *On Charisma and Institution Building*. Chicago: University of Chicago Press.

Elias, Norbert. 1978. *What Is Sociology?* New York: Columbia University Press.

Ember, Melvin. 1983. On the Origin and Extension of the Incest Taboo. In Melvin Ember and Carol R. Ember (eds.), *Marriage, Family, and Kinship*. New Haven: HRAF Press.

Engels, Frederick. 1942 (1884). *The Origin of the Family, Private Property, and the State*. New York: International Publishers.

Evans-Pritchard, E. E. 1948. *The Divine Kingship of the Shilluk of the Nilotic Sudan*. Cambridge: Cambridge University Press.

Faron, Louis. 1956. Araucanian Patri-Organization and the Omaha System. *American Anthropologist* 58:435–456.

Fischer, H. T. 1950. The Concept of Incest in Sumatra. *American Anthropologist* 52:219–224.

Fischer, J. L., et al. 1976. Ponapean Conceptions of Incest. *Journal of the Polynesian Society* 85:199–207.

Fiske, Alan. 1982. Incest Is Gauche, Lineage Adultery Is Taboo. Unpublished Paper Presented at the Annual Meeting of the American Anthropological Association, Washington, D.C.

Flandrin, Jean-Louis. 1979. *Families in Former Times*. Cambridge: Cambridge University Press.

Fleming, Patricia. 1973. The Politics of Marriage among Non-Catholic European Royalty. *Current Anthropology* 14:231–249.

Fortes, Meyer. 1983. *Rules and the Emergence of Society*. London: Royal Anthropological Institute.

Foucault, Michel. 1978. *The History of Sexuality*. Vol. I. New York: Pantheon Books.

Foucault, Michel. 1980. *Power/Knowledge*. New York: Pantheon Books.

Fox, Robin. 1962. Sibling Incest. *British Journal of Sociology* 13:128–150.

Fox, Robin. 1967. "Totem and Taboo" Reconsidered. In Edmund Leach (ed.), *The Structural Study of Myth and Totemism*. London: Tavistock.

Fox, Robin. 1975. *Encounter with Anthropology*. New York: Dell Publishing Company.

Fox, Robin. 1979. Kinship Categories as Natural Categories. In Napoleon Chagnon and William Irons (eds.), *Evolutionary Biology and Human Social Behavior*. North Scituate, Mass.: Duxbury Press.

Fox, Robin. 1980. *The Red Lamp of Incest*. New York: E. P. Dutton.

Fox, Robin. 1983. *Kinship and Marriage*. Cambridge: Cambridge University Press.

Frances, Vera, and Allen Frances. 1976. The Incest Taboo and Family Structure. *Family Process* 15:234–244.

Frazer, James. 1910. *Totemism and Exogamy*. Vol. IV. London: Macmillan.

Frazer, James. 1963 (1922). *The Golden Bough*. London: Macmillan.

Freeman, Derek. 1970. Totem and Taboo: A Reappraisal. In Warner Muensterberger (ed.), *Man and His Culture*. New York: Taplinger Publishing Co.

Freud, Sigmund. 1950. *Totem and Taboo*. New York: W. W. Norton.

Freud, Sigmund. 1955. *The Complete Works of Sigmund Freud*. Vol. III. London: Hogarth Press.

Frost, John. 1974. *A History of the Shilluk of the Southern Sudan*. Unpublished Ph.D. Dissertation. University of California, Santa Barbara.

Gay, Peter. 1984. *Education of the Senses*. New York: Oxford University Press.

Geertz, Clifford. 1983. *Local Knowledge*. New York: Basic Books.

Gephard, Paul, et al. 1965. *Sex Offenders*. New York: Harper and Row.

Goggin, John, and William Sturtevant. 1964. The Calusa. In Ward Goodenough (ed.), *Explorations in Cultural Anthropology*. New York: McGraw-Hill.

Goodall, Jane. 1967. Mother-Offspring Relationship in Free-Ranging Chimpanzees. In Desmond Morris (ed.), *Primate Ethology*. London: Weidenfield and Nicolson.

Goody, Jack. 1969. A Comparative Approach to Incest and Adultery. *British Journal of Sociology* 7:286–305.

Hamilton, W. D. 1963. The Evolution of Altruistic Behavior. *American Naturalist* 97:354–356.

Hamilton, W. D. 1964. The Genetical Evolution of Social Behavior. *Journal of Theoretical Biology* 7:1–52.

Hammond, David, and Charles Jackson. 1958. Consanguinity in a Midwestern United States Isolate. *American Journal of Human Genetics* 10:61–63.

Harris, Marvin. 1971. *Culture, Man, and Nature*. New York: Crowell.

Harris, Marvin. 1975. *Culture, People, and Nature*. New York: Crowell.

Harris, Marvin. 1977. *Cannibals and Kings*. New York: Random House.

Henderson, D. J. 1972. Incest: A Synthesis of Data. *Canadian Psychiatric Association Journal* 17:299–314.

Henderson, D. J. 1975. Incest. In A. M. Freedman et al. (eds.), *Comprehensive Textbook of Psychiatry*, Vol. 2. Baltimore: Williams and Wilkins.

Herdt, Gilbert H. 1981. *Guardians of the Flutes*. New York: McGraw-Hill.

Herman, Judith Lewis. 1981. *Father-Daughter Incest*. Cambridge: Harvard University Press.

Hertier, Francoise. 1982. The Symbolics of Incest and Its Prohibition. In Michael Izard and Pierre Smith (eds.), *Between Belief and Transgression*. Chicago: University of Chicago Press.

Hill, James L. 1974. Peromyscus: Effect of Early Pairing on Reproduction. *Science* 186:1042–1044.

Hocart, A. M. 1970 (1936). *Kings and Councillors*. Chicago: University of Chicago Press.

Hockett, C. F. 1973. *Man's Place in Nature*. New York: McGraw-Hill.

Hoebel, E. Adamson. 1953. An Eighteenth Century Culturalogical Explanation for the Incest Taboo. *American Anthopologist* 55: 280–281.

Hofmayr, W. 1911. *Religion der Schilluk*. Modling, Germany: Anthropos.

Hofmayr, W. 1925. *Die Schilluk*. Modling, Germany: Anthropos.

Hooper, Antony. 1976. "Eating Blood": Tahitian Concepts of Incest. *Journal of the Polynesian Society*. 85:227–241.

Hopkins, Keith. 1980. Brother-Sister Marriage in Roman Egypt. *Comparative Studies in Society and History* 22:303–354.

Howell, P. P. 1944. The Installation of the Shilluk King. *Man* 44: 146–147.

Howell, P. P. 1952a. The Death of Reth Dak Wad Fadiet and the Installation of His Successor: A Preliminary Note. *Man* 52: 102–104.

Howell, P. P. 1952b. The Death and Burial of *reth* Dak *wad* Fadiet of the Shilluk. *Sudan Notes and Records* 33:156–166.

Howell, P. P. 1953. The Election and Installation of Reth Kur Wad Fafiti of the Shilluk. *Sudan Notes and Records* 34:189–203.

Howell, P. P., and W. P. G. Thomson. 1946. The Death of a Reth of the Shilluk and the Installation of His Successor. *Sudan Notes and Records* 27:5–35.

Huntington, Richard. 1978. Bara Endogamy and Incest Prohibition. *Bijdragen tot de Taal-, Land-en Volkenkunde* 134:30–62.

Huntington, Richard, and Metcalf, Peter. 1979. *Celebrations of Death*. New York: Cambridge University Press.

Hussien, F. H. 1971. Endogamy in Egyptian Nubia. *Journal of Bio social Science* 3:251–259.

Huxley, T. H. 1863. *Evidence as to Man's Place in Nature*. London and Edinburgh: Williams and Norgate.

Imanishi, Kinji. 1965. The Origin of the Human Family: A Primatological Approach. In Stuart Altmann (ed.), *Japanese Monkeys*. Atlanta: Published by the Editor.

Irons, William. 1979. Natural Selection, Adaption, and Human Social Behavior. In Napoleon Chagnon and William Irons (eds.), *Evolutionary Biology and Human Social Behavior*. North Scituate, Mass.: Duxbury Press.

Jensen, Gordon. 1973. Human Sexual Behavior in Primate Perspective. In J. Zubin and John Money (eds.), *Contemporary Sexual Behavior*. Baltimore: Johns Hopkins University Press.

Kaffman, Mordecai. 1977. Sexual Standards and the Behavior of the Kibbutz Adolescent. *American Journal of Orthopsychiatry* 47: 207–217.

Kaufmann, J. H. 1965. A Three-Year Study of Mating Behavior in a Free-Ranging Band of Rhesus Monkeys. *Ecology* 46:500–512.

Kettel, David. 1982. Cognition and Contradiction: On the Origin of Incest Taboos and Oedipal Fantasies. *Dialectical Anthropology* 7:31–45.

Khatib-Chahidi, Jane. 1981. Sexual Prohibitions, Shared Space and Fictive Marriages in Shi'ite Iran. In Shirley Ardener (ed.), *Women and Space*. London: Croom Helm.

Kinsey, Alfred, Wardell Pomery, and Clyde Martin. 1948. *Sexual Behavior in the Human Male*. Philadelphia: W. B. Saunders Company.

Kirkpatrick, J. 1972. Some Unexamined Aspects of Childhood Association and Sexual Attraction in the Chinese Minor Marriage. *American Anthropologist* 74:783–784.

Koch, Klaus-Friedrich. 1974. Incest and Its Punishment in Jale Society. *Journal of the Polynesian Society* 83:84–91.

Kohler, Joseph. 1975 (1897). *On the Prehistory of Marriage*. Chicago: University of Chicago Press.

Korbin, Jill (ed.). 1981. *Child Abuse and Neglect*. Berkeley: University of California Press.

Kortmulder, K. 1968. An Ethnological Theory of the Incest Taboo and Exogamy. *Current Anthropology* 9:437–450.

Krige, E. Jensen. 1975. Divine Kingship, Change and Development.

In Meyer Fortes and Sheila Patterson (eds.), *Studies in African Social Anthropology*. London: Academic Press.

Krige, E. Jensen, and J. D. Krige. 1943. *The Realm of a Rain Queen*. London: Oxford University Press.

Kroeber, A. L. 1920. Totem and Taboo: An Ethnologic Psychoanalysis. *American Anthopologist* 22:48–55.

Kroeber, A. L. 1939. Totem and Taboo in Restrospect. *American Journal of Sociology* 55:446–451.

Kroeber, A. L., and Clyde Kluckhohn. 1952. *Culture*. Cambridge: Papers of the Peabody Museum of American Archaeology and Ethnology. V. 65.

Kummer, Hans. 1968. *Social Organization of Hamadryas Baboons*. Chicago: The University of Chicago Press.

Kuper, Hilda, 1947. *An African Aristocracy*. London: Oxford University Press.

Kurland, J. A. 1979. Paternity, Mother's Brother, and Human Sociality. In Napoleon Chagnon and William Irons (eds). *Evolutionary Biology and Human Social Behavior*. North Scituate, Mass.: Duxbury Press.

Labby, David. 1976. Incest as Cannibalism: The Yapese Analysis. *Journal of the Polynesian Society* 85:171–179.

Lancaster, Jane. 1984. Introduction. In Meredith Small (ed.), *Female Primates*. New York: Alan R. Liss.

Leach, Edmund. 1967. Virgin Birth. *Proceedings of the Royal Anthropological Institute of Great Britain and Ireland* 1966: 39–50.

Leach, Edmund, 1969. *Genesis as Myth and Other Essays*. London: Jonathan Cape.

Leach, Edmund. 1976. *Culture and Communication*. Cambridge: Cambridge University Press.

Leach, Edmund, and D. Alan Aycock. 1983. *Structuralist Interpretations of Biblical Myth*. Cambridge: Cambridge University Press.

Letourneau, Charles. 1911. *The Evolution of Marriage*. New York: Walter Scott.

Lévi-Strauss, Claude. 1969. *The Elementary Structures of Kinship*. London: Eyne and Spottiswoode.

Lienhardt, Godfrey. 1954. The Shilluk of the Upper Nile. In Daryll Forde (ed.), *African Worlds*. London: Oxford University Press.

Livingstone, Frank B. 1969. Genetics, Ecology and the Origins of Incest and Exogamy. *Current Anthropology* 10:45–61.

Bibliography 179

Lorenz, Konrad. 1971. Studies in Animal and Human Behavior. Cambridge: Harvard University Press.

Lubbock, John. 1978 (1870). The Origin of Civilization and the Primitive Condition of Man. Chicago: University of Chicago Press.

Lumsden, Charles J., and Edmund O. Wilson. 1981. Genes, Mind, and Culture. Cambridge: Harvard University Press.

Lumsden, Charles J., and Edmund O. Wilson. 1983. Promethean Fire. Cambridge: Harvard University Press.

Lustig, Noel, et al. 1966. Incest: A Family Group Survival Pattern. Archives of General Psychiatry 14:31–40.

Machotka, Pavel, et al. 1967. Incest as a Family Affair. Family Process 6:98–116.

Maisch, Herbert. 1972. Incest. New York: Stein and Day.

Malcolm, Janet. 1983. Annals of Scholarship. The New Yorker. December 5, 1983, pp. 59–152, and December 12, 1983, pp. 60–110.

Malcolm, Janet. 1984. In the Freud Archives. New York: Knopf.

Malinowski, Bronislaw. 1927. Sex and Repression in a Savage Society. London: Routledge and Kegan Paul.

Malinowski, Bronislaw. 1929. The Sexual Life of Savages. New York: Harcourt, Brace and World, Inc.

Marett, R. R. 1932. Faith, Hope and Charity in Primitive Religion. Oxford: Clarendon Press.

Mauss, Marcel. 1979. Sociology and Psychology. London: Routledge and Kegan Paul.

McCabe, Justin. 1983. FBD Marriage: Further Support for the Westermarck Hypothesis of the Incest Taboo? American Anthropologist 85:50–69.

McC. Pastner, Carroll. 1982. The Westermarck Hypothesis and First Cousin Marriage. Unpublished Paper Presented at the Annual Meeting of the American Anthropological Association, Washington, D.C.

McGuire, Michael, and Lowell Getz. 1981. Incest Taboo between Sibling Microtus Ochrogaster. Journal of Mammalogy 62:213–215.

McKusick, Victor. 1964. Foundations of Modern Genetics. Englewood Cliffs: Prentice-Hall.

McKusick, Victor, et al. 1978a. The Distribution of Certain Genes in the Old Order Amish. In Victor McKusick (ed.), Medical Genetics Studies of the Amish. Baltimore: Johns Hopkins University Press.

McKusick, Victor et al. 1978b. Dwarfism in the Amish. In Victor McKusick (ed.), *Medical Genetic Studies of the Amish*. Baltimore: Johns Hopkins University Press.

McLennan, John F. 1970. *Primitive Marriage*. Chicago: University of Chicago Press.

Mead, Margaret. 1968. Incest. In David Sills (ed.), *International Encyclopedia of the Social Sciences*. New York: Collier Macmillan.

Mercer, Patricia. 1971. Shilluk Trade and Politics from the Mid-Seventeenth Century to 1861. *Journal of African History* 12: 407–426.

Middleton, Russel. 1962. A Deviant Case: Brother-Sister and Father-Daughter Marriage in Ancient Egypt. *American Sociological Review* 27:603–611.

Missakian, Elizabeth. 1973. Genealogical Mating Activity in Free-Ranging Groups of Rhesus Monkeys (Macaca Mulatta) on Cayo Santiago. *Behavior* 45:225–241.

Monberg, Torben. 1975. Fathers Were Not Genitors. *Man* 10:34–40.

Montagu, M. F. Ashley. 1956. Editor's Introduction to Robert Briffault and Bronislaw Malinowski, *Marriage: Past and Present*. Boston: Porter Sargent.

Moore, Jim, and Rauf Ali. 1984. Are Dispersal and Inbreeding Avoidance Related? *Animal Behavior* 32:94–112.

Moore, Sally Falk. 1960. Psychological Deterrents to Incest. *American Anthropologist* 62:881–82.

Moore, Sally Falk. 1964. Descent and Symbolic Filiation. *American Anthropologist* 66:1308–1320.

Morgan, Lewis Henry. 1877. *Ancient Society*. New York: Holt.

Morton, N. E. 1961. Morbidity of Children from Consanguineous Marriages. In Arthur Steinberg (ed.). *Progress in Medical Genetics*. New York: Grune and Stratton.

Muldoon, Linda (ed.). n.d. *Incest: Confronting the Silent Crime*. St. Paul: The Minnesota Program for Victims of Sexual Assault.

Munro, P. 1918. Installation of the Ret of the Chol (King of the Shilluks). *Sudan Notes and Records* 1:145–152.

Murdock, George P. 1965. *Social Structure*. New York: The Free Press.

Needham, Rodney. 1962. Notes on Comparative Method and Prescriptive Alliance. *Bijdragen tot de Taal-, Land-en Volkenkunde* 118:160–182.

Needham, Rodney. 1970. Editor's Introduction to A. M. Hocart, *Kings and Councillors*. Chicago: University of Chicago Press.

Needham, Rodney. 1974. *Remarks and Inventions*. London: Tavistock Publications.

Needham, Rodney. 1976. Editor's Introduction to Carl Starcke, *The Primitive Family in Its Origin and Development*. Chicago: The University of Chicago Press.

Needham, Rodney. 1983. *Against the Tranquility of Axioms*. Berkeley: University of California Press.

Neel, J. V. 1958. A Study of Major Congenital Defects in Japanese Children. *American Journal of Human Genetics* 10:398–445.

Packer, C. 1979. Inter-Troop Transfer and Inbreeding Avoidance in Anubis. *Animal Behavior* 27:1–36.

Parker, Seymour. 1976. The Precultural Basis of the Incest Taboo: Toward a Biosocial Theory. *American Anthropologist* 78:285–305.

Parker, Seymour. 1985. Personal Communication.

Parsons, Anne. 1970. Is the Oedipus Complex Universal? In Warner Muensterberger (ed.), *Man and His Culture*. New York: Taplinger Publishing Co.

Parsons, Talcott. 1954. The Incest Taboo in Relation to Social Structure and the Socialization of the Child. *British Journal of Sociology* 5:101–117.

Peters, Joseph. 1976. Children Who Are Victims of Sexual Assault and the Psychology of Offenders. *American Journal of Psychotherapy* 30:398–421.

Pusey, Anne. 1980. Inbreeding Avoidance in Chimpanzees. *Animal Behavior* 28:543–552.

Raglan, Lord. 1940. *Jocasta's Crime*. London: Watts & Co.

Raphling, David, et al. 1967. Incest: A Genealogical Study. *Archives of General Psychiatry* 16:505–511.

Renshaw, Domeena. 1982. *Incest*. Boston: Little, Brown and Company.

Riad, Mohamed. 1956. *The Divine Kingship of the Shilluk and Its Origin*. Unpublished Ph.D. Dissertation. University of Vienna.

Richards, Audrey I. 1969. Keeping the King Divine. *Proceedings of the Royal Anthropological Institute of Great Britain and Ireland for 1968*. London: Royal Anthropological Institute.

Rieff, Philip. 1961. *Freud: The Mind of the Moralist*. Garden City, N.Y.: Doubleday.

Riemer, Svend. 1940. A Research Note on Incest. *American Journal of Sociology* 45:566–575.

Roberts, D. F. 1967. Incest, Inbreeding, and Mental Abilities. *British Medical Journal* 4:336–337.

Rose, Frederick. 1951. More on the Origin of Incest Rules. *American Anthropologist* 53:139–141.

Rosenblatt, Paul C. 1974. Cross Cultural Perspective on Attachment. In Ted L. Huston (ed.), *Foundations of Interpersonal Attraction*. New York: Academic Press.

Rosenzweig, Saul. 1973. Human Sexual Autonomy as an Evolutionary Attainment. In J. Zubin and John Money (eds.), *Contemporary Sexual Behavior*. Baltimore: Johns Hopkins University Press.

Ruffer, Marc. 1921. *Studies in the Palaeopathology of Egypt*. Chicago: University of Chicago Press.

Rush, Florence. 1980. *The Best Kept Secret*. Englewood Cliffs: Prentice-Hall, Inc.

Sade, Donald. 1968. Inhibition of Son-Mother Mating Among Free-Ranging Rhesus Monkeys. In Jules Masserman (ed.), *Animal and Human*. New Yord: Grune & Stratton.

Sahlins, Marshall. 1959. The Social Life of Monkeys, Apes and Primitive Man. In James N. Spuhler (ed.), *The Evolution of Man's Capacity for Culture*. Detroit: Wayne State Press.

Sahlins, Marshall D. 1960. The Origin of Society. *Scientific American* 203:76–86.

Sahlins, Marshall. 1976. *The Use and Abuse of Biology*. Ann Arbor: The University of Michigan Press.

Schaller, George. 1964. *The Year of the Gorilla*. Chicago: University of Chicago Press.

Schneider, David M. 1976. The Meaning of Incest. *Journal of the Polynesian Society* 85:149–169.

Schull, W. J. 1958. Empirical Risks in Consanguineous Marriages. *American Journal of Human Genetics* 10:294–343.

Schull, W. J. 1972. Genetic Implications of Population Breeding Structure. In G. A. Harrison and A. J. Boyce (eds.), *The Structure of Human Populations*. Oxford: Clarendon.

Schull, W. J., and J. V. Neel. 1965. *The Effects of Inbreeding on Japanese Children*. New York: Harper and Row.

Schull, W. J., and J. V. Neel. 1972. The Effects of Parental Consanguinity and Inbreeding in Hirado, Japan. *American Journal of Human Genetics* 24:425–453.

Schultz, Le Roy G. 1979. *The Sexual Victimology of Youth*. Unpublished Ms.

Seemanová, Eva. 1971. A Study of Children of Incestuous Matings. *Human Heredity* 21:108–128.

Segner, L. L. 1968. *Two Studies of the Incest Taboo*. Unpublished Ph.D. Dissertation. University of Texas.

Seligman, C. G., and Brenda Z. Seligman. 1932. *Pagan Tribes of the Nilotic Sudan*. London: Routledge and Kegan Paul Ltd.

Seligman, Brenda Z. 1950. The Problem of Incest and Exogamy: A Restatement. *American Anthropologist* 52:305–316.

Shepher, Joseph. 1971. Mate Selection Among Second Generation Kibbutz Adolescents and Adults. *Archives of Sexual Behavior* 1:293–307.

Shepher, Joseph. 1983. *Incest*. New York: Academic Press.

Shils, Edward. 1965. Charisma, Order, and Status. *American Sociological Review* 30:199–213.

Slater, Mariam K. 1959. Ecological Factors in the Origin of Incest. *American Anthropologist* 61:1042–1059.

Slatis, H. M., et al. 1958. Consanguineous Marriages in the Chicago Region. *American Journal of Human Genetics* 10:446–464.

Sloane, Paul, and Eva Karpinski. 1942. Effects of Incest on Participants. *American Journal of Orthopsychiatry* 12:666–673.

Smith, Alfred, and John Kennedy. 1960. The Extension of Incest Taboos in Woleai, Micronesia. *American Anthropologist* 62:643–647.

Smith, W. Robertson. 1963 (1903). *Kinship and Marriage in Early Arabia*. Boston: Beacon Press.

Spiro, Melford. 1958. *Children of the Kibbutz*. Cambridge: Harvard University Press.

Spiro, Melford. 1968. Virgin Birth, Parthenogenesis, and Physiological Paternity. *Man* 3:242–261.

Spiro, Melford. 1982. *Oedipus in the Trobriands*. Chicago: University of Chicago Press.

Starcke, Carl. 1976 (1888). *The Primitive Family in Its Origin and Development*. Chicago: The University of Chicago Press.

Starin, E. D. 1981. Monkey Moves. *Natural History* 90:36–43.

Stern, Curt. 1973. *Principles of Human Genetics*. San Francisco: Freeman.

Storr, Anthony. 1972. *Human Destructiveness*. London: Chatto-Heinemann.

Strabo. 1939. *The Geography of Strabo*. Book 4. London: William Heinemann.

Stroup, Timothy (ed.). 1982. *Edward Westermarck*. Helsinki: Acta Philosophica Fennica.

Stroup, Timothy. 1984. Edward Westermarck: A Reappraisal. *Man* 19:575–592.

Sturtevant, William C. 1981. Royal Incest: A Bibliographic Note. *American Ethnologist* 8:186.

Sutter, J. 1958. *Recherches sur les effets de la consanguinite chez l'homme*. Lons-le-Saunier: Declume Press.

Sutter, J., and L. Tabah. 1951. Effets des marriages consanguins sur la descendance. *Population* 6:59–82.

Swartz, Marc, and D. K. Jordan. 1976. *Culture: The Anthropological Perspective*. New York: Wiley.

Talman, Yonia. 1964. Mate Selection in Collective Settlements. *American Sociological Review* 29:491–508.

Teilhard de Chardin, Pierre. 1965. *The Phenomenon of Man*. New York: Harper and Row.

Thomas, Keith. 1983. *Man and the Natural World*. New York: Pantheon Books.

Tokuda, K. 1961–62. A Study of Sexual Behavior in the Japanese Monkey Troop. *Primates* 3:1–40.

Turner, Victor. 1962. Three Symbols of Passage in Ndembu Circumcision Ritual. In Max Gluckman (ed.), *Essays on the Ritual of Social Relations*. Manchester: Manchester University Press.

Tylor, E. B. 1889. On a Method of Investigating the Development of Institutions: Applied to Laws of Marriage and Descent. *Journal of the Royal Anthropological Institute* 18:245–269.

van den Berghe, Pierre, and David Barash. 1977. Inclusive Fitness and Family Structure. *American Anthropologist* 79:809–823.

van den Berghe, Pierre, and Gene Mesher. 1980. Royal Incest and Inclusive Fitness. *American Ethnologist* 7:300–317.

van den Berghe, Pierre, and Gene Mesher. 1981. Royal Incest: A Reply to Sturtevant. *American Ethnologist* 8:187–188.

Van Gennep, Arnold. 1960. *The Rites of Passage*. Chicago: University of Chicago Press.

Veit, Peter G. 1982. Gorilla Society. *Natural History* 91:48–59.

Vivelo, Frank. 1978. *Cultural Anthropology Handbook*. New York: McGraw-Hill.

Wake, C. Staniland. 1967 (1889). *The Development of Marriage and Kinship*. Chicago: University of Chicago Press.

Walens, Stanley. 1981. *Feasting with Cannibals*. Princeton: Princeton University Press.

Wallace, Edwin. 1983. *Freud and Anthropology*. New York: International Universities Press.

Wallis, W. 1950. The Origin of Incest Rules. *American Anthropologist* 52:277–279.

Washburn, Sherwood, and Irven DeVore. 1961. Social Behavior of Baboons and Early Man. In Sherwood Washburn (ed.), *Social Life of Early Man*. Chicago: Aldine Publishing Company.

Washburn, Sherwood, and C. Lancaster. 1968. The Evolution of Hunting. In Richard Lee and Irven DeVore (eds.), *Man the Hunter*. Chicago: Aldine Publishing Co.

Weber, Gay. 1974. Science and Society in Nineteenth Century Anthropology. *History of Science* 12:260–283.

Weber, Max. 1968. *On Charisma and Institution Building*. Chicago: University of Chicago Press.

Westermarck, Edward. 1914. *Marriage Ceremonies in Morocco*. London: Macmillan & Co.

Westermarck, Edward. 1916. *The Moorish Conception of Holiness* (*Baraka*). Helsingfors, Finland: Helsingfors Centraetryckeri.

Westmarck, Edward. 1921 (1894). *The History of Human Marriage*. Three Volumes. London: Macmillan.

Westmarck, Edward. 1926. *Ritual and Belief in Morocco*. Vols. I and II. London: Macmillan.

Westermarck, Edward. 1929. *Memories of My Life*. New York: Macaulay.

Westermarck, Edward. 1931. *Wit and Wisdom in Morocco: A Study of Native Proverbs*. New York: Liverwright.

Westermarck, Edward. 1936. *The Future of Marriage in Western Civilization*. New York: Macmillan.

Westermarck, Edward. 1968 (1926). *A Short History of Human Marriage*. New York: Humanities Press.

Westermarck, Edward. 1971 (1906–08). *The Origin and Development of the Moral Ideas*. Two Volumes. Freeport: Books for Libraries Press.

White, Leslie A. 1948. The Definition and Prohibition of Incest. *American Anthropologist* 50:416–435.

White, Leslie A. 1975. *The Concept of Cultural Systems*. New York: Columbia University Press.

Wilson, Edmund O. 1975. *Sociobiology*. Cambridge: Harvard University Press.

Wilson, Edmund O. 1978. *On Human Nature*. Cambridge: Harvard University Press.

Wilson, Monica. 1959. *Divine Kings and the "Breath of Men."* Cambridge University Press.

Wilson, Peter J. 1963. Incest: A Case Study. *Social and Economic Studies* 12:200–209.

Wilson, Peter J. 1975. The Promising Primate. *Man* 10:5–20.

Wilson, Peter J. 1980. *Man the Promising Primate.* New Haven: Yale University Press.

Wolf, Arthur P. 1966. Childhood Association, Sexual Attraction, and the Incest Taboo: A Chinese Case. *American Anthropologist* 68:883–898.

Wolf, Arthur P. 1968. Adopt a Daughter-in-Law, Marry a Sister: A Chinese Solution to the Problem of the Incest Taboo. *American Anthropologist* 70:864–874.

Wolf, Arthur P. 1970. Childhood Association and Sexual Attraction: A Further Test of the Westermarck Hypothesis. *American Anthropologist* 72:503–515.

Wolf, Arthur, and C. S. Huang. 1980. *Marriage and Adoption in China, 1845–1945.* Stanford: Stanford University Press.

Wolf, Margery. 1968. *The House of Lim.* Englewood Cliffs: Prentice-Hall.

Wolfe, Linda. 1984. Japanese Macaque Sexual Behavior. In Meredith Small (ed.), *Female Primates.* New York: Alan R. Liss.

Yamaguchi, Masao. 1972. Kingship as a System of Myth. *Diogenes* 77: 43–70.

Yorukoglu, Atalay, and John Kemph. 1966. Children Not Severely Damaged by Incest with a Parent. *Journal of the American Academy of Child Psychiatry* 5:111–124.

Young, Michael W. 1966. The Divine Kingship of the Jukun: A Re-Evaluation of Some Theories. *Africa* 36:135–153.

Zuckerman, S. 1932. *The Social Life of Monkeys and Apes.* London: Kegan Paul, Trench, Trubner & Co., Ltd.

Zuckerman, S. 1933. *Functional Affinities of Man, Monkeys, and Apes.* New York: Harcourt, Brace and Company.

Index

DATE DUE